On the
Green Carpet

On the Green Carpet

by ROBERT P. TRISTRAM COFFIN
George Elliston Professor of Poetry
UNIVERSITY OF CINCINNATI

KENNIKAT PRESS/PORT WASHINGTON, N. Y.

TO
MIRIAM SMALL
TRUE-BLUE
COLLEAGUE AND FRIEND
IN WELLS
IN MAINE
IN LITERATURE AND LIFE

Acknowledgments

This book grew out of some of the lectures the writer gave in inaugurating the George Elliston Poetry Foundation at the University of Cincinnati, in 1951; and the author is most grateful to the University for giving him this opportunity to develop these ideas on the poet's art.

A very special debt of gratitude, too, the writer owes to the Macmillan Company for their kind consent to his using in this book many poems of his copyrighted by them.

The lines from Housman's poems on pages 42-43 are from *The Collected Poems of A. E. Housman.* Copyright, 1922, 1940, by Henry Holt and Company, Inc. Copyright, 1936, 1950, by Barclays Bank, Ltd. Used by permission of the publishers, to whom the author extends his thanks.

Finally, the author wishes to thank the following magazines for transferring to him copyrights on poems of his they have recently published: the *Atlantic Monthly, Ladies' Home Journal, New York Herald Tribune, Saturday Evening Post,* and *Saturday Review of Literature.*

Contents

Chapter		Page
I	THE GREEN CARPET	13
II	THE SALVATION WHICH IS THE NORTH	53
III	THE YEOMANLY SHAKESPEARE	91
IV	THE NEW ENGLAND GREEN	127
V	GREEN MAINE	165
VI	CATHEDRALS OF THE NORTH	203
VII	FOOTPRINTS ON THE GREEN	239

~ 1 ~

THE GREEN CARPET

I. The Green Carpet

Across many years, I can still hear that old ring-game song of my childhood. I can recall the very tune to it, even. We boys and girls stood in a circle holding hands—Oh, many and many a time, it seems—on the green grass. It was usually dandelion time. Multitudes of small suns were blazing under our feet. Maybe our boy-feet were bare for the first time of the year. Anyway, it was some memorable peak to our year. We had company. There were more children there than merely brothers and sisters. It was a great occasion. We were in society. We were on our gilt-edge behavior. Our ears were scrubbed, and we were bathed all over in a special radiance. We had our feet on the wide green world. Even we boys felt tremblings. For girls were there, and each of us was about to choose one for his special own. We were singing. We were swinging our joined hands. We were singing in a ring.

> On the green carpet here we stand,
> Take your true-love by the hand.

Of course we did not know we were playing a very ancient game, a game with deadly earnest in it, a bread-and-butter game, a game of life, a game for keeps. We had our feet in religion and old poetry. We were playing at a game which, if you followed it far enough back, had the sound of breath and death in it, of once and for all, of taking and giving in

[13]

marriage and the procreation and perpetuation of new rings of bright-haired boys and girls like us on down through the dark unwilling inertias of the years like circles of fire. We were playing with light. We were playing with fire.

We did not know a thing about all this at the time—did not know it as a fact. Yet I swear on my honor as a poet we sensed it—knew it as fancy, as a whole uncut cloth of conviction, as the good shrewd guess children always make when they are deep in joy. That was the reason we tingled and blushed, felt shy and backward and yet bold and forward in the same breath, ran hot and cold, fire and ice. And there the fires of the small sons of the sun lit our feet in the grass. There we were in a Druid ring. There was the green color of life on our feet. We felt ourselves, without the words for it, on the edge of the vast.

The play-song we were singing sloped off quickly into the choosing of partners:

> Choose the one that you love best
> Before you close your eyes to rest.

The song grew raucous:

> Oh, what a horrible choice you made!
> Don't you wish you'd longer stayed!
> Give her a kiss and send her away,
> And tell her to call some other day.

It was the heavy-handed hilarity of childhood, the let-down of plain fact.

Yet, just for that slender instant before we chose our rural true-loves, we had held our breaths deep in us and had felt the vast.

In that old folk-song we sang then, in its beginning at least, there *was* the vast, surely. Trust any folk-form to get down to essential form. Euclid, I like to say, may fail us out among the curving vastness of nebular space. Physics may change from century to century, universe to universe. But the geometry of folk-lore, founded not on fallible yardsticks and dead instruments of steel and lead, but on living cells of memory and on the memory that passes from father to son to son, a geometry founded on the will to believe, which is another name for poetry, is a geometry that does not change, a geometry a man can trust. Chronicles go out of date, wars change their weapons; but a man bound for tomorrow's war and bidding goodbye to his infant son had better take off his cap with tall wings on it, so his small son will know him as his father and put out his hands to him, to be taken up and loved for the last time. That is good advice, not out of history, but out of Homer.

That simple small song of my childhood had a great deal under its innocence. It had more rhythms than the rhythms of dancing feet and of choosing mates. It had the circle, which is the figure of holiness, not only under the Round Table but under Stonehenge and the Rollright Stones. It had the geometry of all religions in it. We, with our small hands, were joining hands with the Druids and Hindus, the Cretans and Chaldeans. And that little play pattern of ours had in it the green carpet.

Over the turning continents of the globe, over the turning centuries of time, there is one fast color that does not change.

[15]

On the Green Carpet

It is the color of the returning leaves and grasses, the hue of Spring, color of immortality, color of Proserpine. The color of green. That carpet that rolls out anew each year over the earth, woven on the looms of the sun and moon, the winds, the clouds, and the sea, never fades out in the sun, never runs in the rain. As long as that carpet is there, there will be life on it, dancing of reiterated generations, and singing like that we children were doing that day years ago.

Metaphor, mother of poetry, was in that childhood folksong of ours. Metaphor, mother of life. For the metaphor of the sun is the daisy in the grass; the metaphor of a father's holding his small son's hand in the dark grows and becomes Jehovah; the good neighbor grows a metaphor for God. The hunger to move is the metaphor that creates fins and feet and wings.

It is out of this folk-metaphor of the green carpet that I propose to build this book. A small beginning; but it is a beginning in metaphor, just as this useful metaphor of a *chair* of poetry is. It is a good beginning, I think. For this particular carpet is the synonym for all life on this planet. This color green is the secret of man's best hope for survival and perpetuity.

Green, the color of the country! Even the urban Horace celebrates it, and the Horatian Herrick, unwilling poet of the Devon rural year, finds in the country his one sure way towards immortality. *Rura cano!* It is a better theme than *arma virumque cano*. For arms and men grow old and tire. Rust takes the finest Damascus steel, death the strongest Hectors. Rust and rot and restless change take them all. Devices and towers fall. Cities and philosophies and etiquettes

[16]

and laws are broken by time, *edax rerum*. Yet still the wild rose comes on, never later than July; the seasons keep the slow sure rhythms of their dances, the sun climbs up the steep eastern earth fresh with dew, and the robin builds a new house to give an old man a new hope in his ruined portico.

Charity we have with us always in the animals that must die by violence, looking out on the world with forgiveness, beforetimes, as their very eyes. Piety is preached to us by westering faces of sunflowers. Pity we can learn wherever this Summer's nestling huddles blind in his nest under the gale. Emperors and ambition subside into flat and wormy chronicles; but still the high-headed storms come on out of the west. White-headed Zeus fades into fable; but the white heads of the godly thunder rise up young as ever around all our common little years. Precept and metaphor, metonymy and magic, golden rules of dandelions and green laws of grass are all about us on the open emerald earth, wherever clouds gather, the sun shines, the moon makes haloes in pine needles, or the rain makes dimples in the dust. Wherever trees and grass are man can find confidence, comfort, and belief. The cure for atheism is a green year with the wheels of the seasons rolling over plowland and forest. The cynic is the son of the city. He can flourish only on pavements. Despair and disintegration depend on brick and mortar. Under the depending grapes only hope and trust can be found. The fall of a city may be in vain; but Jonah found Jehovah under his stricken gourd. There was never a better example of trust than the minute humming-bird turning his three inches of Summer southward into the teeth of great continental gales, travelling bee-line to the perpetual Summer of the Tropics.

On every northern hill in April, the airy skin of the snake makes Easter a fact.

If miracles and mystery are the nurses of faith, if we are happy only when we make our smallness and weakness foci of majesty and infinity, then the country is the right place for us to find our strength in and to see men's faces lighted up by Providence.

Who hath cleft a channel for the waterflood,
Or a way for the lightning of the thunder;
To cause it to rain on a land where no man is;
On the wilderness, wherein there is no man;
To satisfy the waste and desolate ground,
And to cause the tender grass to spring forth?
Hath the rain a father?
Or who hath begotten the drops of dew?
Out of whose womb came the ice?
And the hoary frost of heaven, who hath gendered it? . . .
Who provideth for the raven his prey,
When his young ones cry unto God? . . .
Who hath sent out the wild ass free?
Or who hath loosed the bonds of the swift ass,
Whose home I have made the wilderness,
And the salt land his dwelling-place?
He scorneth the tumult of the city,
Neither heareth he the shoutings of the driver.
The range of the mountains is his pasture,
And he searcheth after every green thing.

The good green of that carpet I stood on as a child is the green under the best poetry in the world. The country has been the cradle of the happy and sad impulses that have kept us going on courageously these thousands of years, through changing economics, shifting politics, crumbling religions, the cruelties of forgetfulness, the wrong roads of smallness of mind and hardness of heart, pride, and the corroding canker of inertia. As sure as Spring, there always has been hope.

> When green buds hang in the elm like dust
> And sprinkle the lime like rain,
> Forth I wander, forth I must,
> And drink of life again.

If we turn slow with age, there are this year's long-legged colts to remind us that youth is forever. If we grow sleek in prosperity, the Autumn gale that wastes the golden leaves in the mire warns us in time; a light frost turns us from sin to the economy of virtue; and our brief Summers make us more in love with the short songs of birds.

Poetry, which is life in the act, is still best caught in the act where it started, in the enduring analogies of man and the setting sun, the candle of the Creator on the eastern waves of the sea, man and the storm and calm, and the quiet and crying of birds. Ages before science guessed at evolution, in our poems we ran brotherly with the slim deer and heard a cousinly voice in the baying hounds. We knew our mother Aphrodite in the fluted seashell, guessed at love brooding over the ocean, and heard ourselves answered by kinsmen in the sibilant words of the pine and the oak. Meteorology begat mythology, mythology taught brotherhood through all the forms of life. Myth and metaphor made us the poets we are.

And it is still but a step, even in these late, iron years, back to the green carpet on which we danced in the childhood of our race, in the genesis of our poetry. One step to salvation. One needs but to go to the first open field full of the sprinkled suns in dandelioned May, to look up at the first tree with a bluebird in it, lift up one's eyes to the nearest hill or the first cloud. Arachne unrolls her story at our town-house's eaves. Proserpina drops her flowers on town commons. Rain and wind, night and sunlight, running water and sibilant leaves are at all the next turns in the road. The poems, the metaphors, are still all around us. The humming-bird revolves his wings and floats still and feasts under our town-window; night-hawks sigh and fall like sad arrows down through our city twilights. However intricate and elaborate the steel cocoon we build around us, the old mother of metaphor is but inches away. The eagle and sea-hawk wheel beside the plane; the squadroned pelicans put our most involved airplane maneuvers to the blush. The green carpet still unrolls its salvation to the foot of our doorsteps. It is but a step to poetry everywhere.

There are just as many clouds now as in Shelley's day. There are as many lakes as in Wordsworth's time. Trees are still chief citizens of earth in number.

For myself, I am thankful that I have been very lucky all my life and never had to live in cities for long. The city I am living in now is the largest I have lived in; and even here the facts of hills and the fact of a lordly river are every day, every way, in our eyes. The nearest to a city I have lived in for long was Oxford, in England. But Oxford then was an overgrown market-town; the green life was never far away. The green carpet was unrolled down the High and the Corn twice a week. I had to walk my new bicycle through Berkshire sheep and Jersey heifers; I had to step over pigs to get into Duke Humfrey's part of the Bodleian. I was lucky then. I have been so since. I have never wanted for a poem at any time. I have had only to look around me.

Now as a historian of poetry I must confess there is another kind of poetry, and a major and marvellous kind, that stems from the cities. There is the great civic poetry of Virgil. And Virgil, the urban, is, it may be, the greatest poet we have seen. Behind his best lines—and they have a way of being best the oftenest of any poet—is citizenship. Virgil is one of the architects of our civilization; his genius is built like the Roman law itself into the civics of the Roman Empire and the graduated obediences of the mediaeval church. Order, decorum, dependence, dependability, responsibility of the parts to the whole—these Roman virtues, along with the Roman sense of justice, are virtues to be learned in the city, surely. Virgil learned them from a Rome becoming a world-state. He declares clearly, in the bronze of his verses, that other states can better develop the arts; but Rome's art is to be the architecture of civics: the subordination of the proud and strong to the state, the architecture of justice for men and nations:

Tu regere imperio populos, Romane, memento
(Hae tibi erunt artes) pacisque imponere morem,
Parcere subiectis et debellare superbos.

Virgil looks forward over two thousand years, over the League of Nations, over our United Nations, and to whatever stronger world assembly, once the nations have resigned their sovereignties to his Roman ideal, may spring in the years to come out of these gropings towards federation. The poet Virgil writes the poetry of community. And that is a great poetry. It is as if the martyred mythical Troy, the city state, had had its final triumph over the Greek pastoral, piscatorial, and agricultural societies by overthrowing them all and sinking all their bitter independences and individualities into the ideal of a harmony transcending all the arts, all the nationalities, all separate cultures and religions, a harmony of foliated obediences building up to a supreme obedience to a community flawless as a divine one, proof against the corrosions of time, the ethics of decay, and the chaos of growth. A vast dream, a great poem; though, it may be, a poem of a vast death. It has its nobilities, though, its splendors. Its shining forums and arches are extensions of white, marble Rome. This poetry of the final citizenship grew from the city certainly.

Over the centuries since Virgil, in cities even larger than Rome, this urban poetry has had its celebrants. There is Ben Jonson in the seventeenth-century London that was becoming England itself, Boileau in a France becoming Paris, Dryden and Pope in the London that *had* become England entire.

The themes of the city poetry are great themes: Decorum, proportion, the *aurea mediocritas* of Horace, the castigation of eccentricity by Juvenal, Ben Jonson, and Dryden; the science and art of conversation the morality of compromise, equity, probity, justice, association, fellowship, taste, the ethics of agreement on the right ways to the good and the beautiful—community. These are great subjects.

Yet note that that great architect of this poetry of the city,

Virgil, was also a poet of the rural virtues. Indeed one of the first great poets of them and one of the best. Virgil was poet of the civics, as it were, of the calendar, the justice of the well-cared-for crops. The probity of the oxen and the well-filled ear are as much his matter as the manifest destiny of the pious, empire-creating Aeneas. With his agrarian north in the marrow of his bones, Virgil could not forget that civics were also to be learned in the beehive and the ox-stall. And this other, northern but warmer Virgil saves the cool, judicial, urban Roman from what might have become such a pure, crystalline but cold geometry as the uninitiated mind finds in Dante's Roman, topmost tier to the mediaeval universe. When the farmer Virgil speaks, the good estate of man's estate glows the more for this mind full of the fragrance of honey and roses and the breath of kine.

For there is, as I shall try to show, an equity of the green pastures, a probity of still waters as well as an equity and probity of towns. There is a lovelier kind of community than any the tallest and whitest cities can teach taught by the birds and beasts, an economy and civics in the seasons of the year and the times of day and night; an economy in aliveness of deer and snakes and winds. It is inculcated by the innocence and confidences of young calves and young country boys and girls. Decorum can be taught by columned porticos and clean squares and streets; but it shines even more convincingly from the honeycomb of the hive and the right sequences of seed and flower and fruit. The green carpet has its citizens, too, and they are good ones. And they do not so quickly go out of date as the citizens of Jonson's London or Virgil's Rome. They are the most enduring citizens of the

[23]

world. They are with us yet as they were in the time of Hesiod. There are communities in the grasses and the Summer trees older than Ur and Babylon, and more powerful teachers of economy than the economists of our day. The measurements of the good man were known and tabulated in *Genesis* and Homer and the countrified *Psalms;* they have not greatly changed at this present. A good husbandman has a wide wisdom in the weather, patience like that in the seeds and seasons, the dignity of strength like that in the ox; the good husbandman in *Proverbs* is a good pattern of the countryman Wordsworth celebrated in his Lake District and Frost celebrates today on Vermont's stony farms. He does not go out of fashion; he is not remade by machines. The colors of the country are fast colors. The justice of the country is a lasting green thing.

The good man is seen at his best against blue sky and the backdrop of seasons. Now in our time as in the times of Abraham and Jacob and David. For a man has in his narrow bones more of the stars and the sun and the grass and the cattle than of brick and mortar, the wheel, the cog, and the coin. Country living, even with tractors and airplanes mingled into its economy, is the best living, still. It is the life of the most essential rhythms. Old age looks better on the farm than in the city; the white of hair goes more decently with the ripened wheat and the snow than it goes with the white of marble. Youth seems more like youth when it shines and is seen in the youthful corn. Lovely complexions and manners are better set off by apple blossoms and sunlight of May than by any man-made illuminations. In spite of all

[24]

our progress these two centuries, what Cowper said—whatever word or idea one cares to substitute for deity—is still true,

God made the country, and man made the town.

This is, I hold, an axiom and the truth. We have always known it and inwardly believed it, whatever our intellects may have tried at different times to concoct as a substitute. Country life is the essential life, whatever sneers the satirists, city men to a man, have turned upon the rustic and the bucolic.

This truth that country living is the good living is so simply apparent that it has struck us, in sophisticated times like the eighteenth century and this twentieth, as naïve. We want truth which is involved and hard to come at, contorted and complex and intricately articulated, vermiculated with doubts and cloudy crucifixions. We want to suffer our poetry, poetize our sufferings; and anything as simple as the green pasture, the goodness of the good shepherd, and the loveliness of still waters is too common for us. It is archaic. It is a myth.

But remark how deep and mystic and persistent that old myth, that common truth, has been! The Golden Age and the dream of the good pastoral life have been with us from the beginnings of our literature. Anything so tough and lasting must have the truth in it. We have always suspected there was evil in coins and affluence; that there were virtue and health and happiness in apples and wheat; that the cottage was a better school of virtue than the palace; that towns made men callous and cruel, but pastures made men broad and kind; that the blue and green of sky and leaf were good colors, and artificial dyes were not; that trade soiled men's hands while plowing cleaned them. We have always known that the working of iron led to wars as the working of wood led to peace. We have always known these axioms. They are not new discoveries today. The poets have always been telling us these truths. The Psalmist and Lucretius, Ovid, Tibullus, and Virgil, Blake and Burns, Whittier and Frost.

> *Nondum caeruleas pinus contemserat undas,*
> *Effusum ventis praebueratque sinum.* . . .
> *Non domus ulla foras habuit; non fixus in agris,*
> *Qui regeret certis finibus arva, lapis*
> *Ipsae mella dabant quercus, ultroque ferebunt*
> *Obvia securis ubera lactis oves.*
> *Non acies, non ira fuit, non bella, nec ensem*
> *Immiti saevus duxerat arte faber.*

Our Christian religion started, as did most other religions, out on this green carpet under the sun and stars, out among sheepfolds under the wide Arabian skies, among lonely country men. Loneliness, nurse of poetry, is also nurse of religion.

So the myth of the Age of Innocence of the world has persisted; of that time before man's covetousness and pride and luxury had made him dye his wool with Tyrian blue, build up cities and plow up the oceans with ships for wealth, work the hard ore of earth into his hardened heart, for the sake of gain, for the sake of heaping up wealth that he must harden his heart to keep.

It all sounds, of course, to sophisticated ears like a child's ring-game, choosing-up verses, a song of childhood:

[26]

The Green Carpet

On the green carpet here we stand,
Take your true-love by the hand.

As if the grass were anything like a carpet! As if there were
anything so simple and plain as a true-love instead of the
slimy crawl of Freudian *libido!*

As a fact, it happens that the dream, the myth is the truth,
and the Freudian dream a malicious and deadly libel of fact.
Most of the world's poetry is there to prove it so. A thousand
years of sublimation of sex in the Middle Ages. If these are
not enough for conviction, if the shout of the poet, if the cry
of the steel soldier on horseback, *"Dieu et ma dame!"* cannot
prove this, then there are the small daisies of the field, the
little suns down in the humble grass, the mysterious shyness
and gentleness of a god in the timorous but kindly deer, to
testify to it; and the joined cry of these can shake the earth
with eloquence. A hopeful infant bird opening its bill to the
hawk for its food proves that Isaiah and Virgil guessed right,
guessed the future in looking back into a Golden Age when
the child put his hand upon the viper's hole, and took no
hurt, the lion and the lamb lay down together, swords turned
plowshares, and the green carpet joined all men of good will
in one fellowship the world around; as if this might happen
far ahead somewhere on what Lucretius calls the coasts of
light. The future in the past, as poetry sings it always shall
be, time being obliterated as the monstrosity and lie that time
is.

There is always the example of the Horatian and urban
Herrick's escape from the sure death of time and the sure
death of the city to the salvation of the green carpet of the

countryside. Londoner born and bred, worshipper of Ben Jonson, Herrick loved the city of the Van Dyck Cavaliers, the courtly city of Lawes and Henrietta Maria as few men have ever loved anything. It was a London of laces and light loves, the domes of Inigo Jones, the strings of Lanière and Ferabosco, and the velvet masques of Saint Ben. But it was also death. For the Court of Charles the First was a doomed place; the umbers and silvers of Van Dyck would fade in the fierce light of the iron years to come; the Julias and Lucastas of Cheapside, of Sir John Suckling and Sir Richard Lovelace, for all the gold dust sprinkled on their hair, were too fragile and perishable to last in the heavy age of pikes and Parliaments and sober business. Marooned among the warty rocks of incivil Devonshire, Robert Herrick cursed his luck in being away from London, deplored his lack of city subjects, of fans and laces and light amours, the thistledown of Cavalier gaiety. He cursed the "salvages" of uncouth Devon. He had to write about what he had, though, in Devon; so he wrote about the wind-blown Devon girls, beanfields in blossom, the hock-carts of the husbandmen, marigolds closing with the sun, the calendar of the country year, rural Chloes and Celias, milkmaids, and tanned

> sons of Summer, by whose toil
> We are the lords of wine and oil.

Herrick was weaned away from the city gods to rustic deities. He had to confess he never had written so much or so well in London as here on the green carpet where daffodils and violets became sisters to Corinna and other lovely girls.

[28]

The Green Carpet

I sing of brooks, of blossoms, birds, and bowers,
Of April, May, of June, and July flowers.
I sing of Maypoles, hock-carts, wassails, wakes,
Of bridegrooms, brides, and of their bridal-cakes.
I write of youth, of love, and have access
By these to sing of cleanly wantonness.

And Robert Herrick's themes saved him. For the cloth of
daffodils is still bright, the cloth of the rural year is unfaded
green and blue and golden still. The brilliant colors of
seventeenth-century London, Van Dyck's slender ladies, the
lutes strummed on the leads under the city moon, the wit and
gaiety of all the other Cavalier poetry are all archaeology
now, a handful of dust in old books. But Herrick lives on
in harvest time, with the garnering of sheaves, with the ever-
renewing calendar of the country. As long as there are farmers and shepherds and the Spring, *The Hesperides* will be a
green and good book. Herrick's green themes saved him,
alone among the Cavaliers, from oblivion. Herrick has escaped, against his original will, into eternity. For May and
daffodils, youth and rosebuds last, and they happen to be
little brothers and sisters of the suns and the nebulae.

Even the homeliest and humblest details of the good green
life, as Herrick discovered, have the quality of eternity and
infinity in them. So I myself have found in my experience as
a poet. Hammers and plows link mankind across the expanding disasters of our long history. They join China and
Egypt with the Western World. Good shapes, shaped by
myriads of hard, working hands, they pass the borders of
nations and go on after the nations fall; they outlast empires.
Weather vanes, in the iconography of farming and fishing

life have come to be as holy as the Cross. They have pointed
the way to salvation wherever men have sailed the furrows
with their plows or the sea with their ships. They are good
iconography.

They wanted a cross in place of the weather vane,
They planned to take the church's arrow down,
The times were full of freer ideas now,
They wanted to be like churches in the town.

The cross was really what the churches meant;
Their grandparents were men of narrow mind.
One farmer heard them, and his heart stood still,
Tears and anger made him suddenly blind.

Why, men for years, good men for generations
Had lifted up their eyes because they must
Know where the wind stood when they went to fish
Or plow the land. Vanes were good things to trust.

The church spire was the highest point they had,
It stood above the highest balsam hill,
It sensed the danger in the upper air
When the Odd-Fellows' roof was in the still.

They had not thought of death and agony,
They had thought God was guardian of good hay,
Of coming home, to bring the children food,
With boatfuls of silver herring from the bay.

The plowman sent his little boy to see
If wind stood in a quarter that was fair,
And many a woman looked up to the church,
With men off on the sea, as though at prayer.

The Green Carpet

The lobstering man said, "Sonny, run and look
How she stands." The small boy, out of breath,
Came shouting shrill, "She's backing round no'theast!"
And saved his sire a forty-fathom death.

They had no right to do this godless thing!
Why, this was turning their old folks out of their graves!
A man was nearest God when, like a child,
He turned to God to know the wind and waves.

A common, homely man and this tool that anticipates the
storms and feels out the coming rain happen to come together, and there you have a timeless poem, as I did:

A man should choose with careful eye
The things to be remembered by.

When I was knee-high to a man,
My father hired Tom McCann.

Tom's days were beanrows without end
And rotting shingles still to mend.

But one blue day the man carved out
An arrow clean as a small boy's shout.

He set up near where God may be
His arrow on a tall pine tree.

The years that broke his willing heart
Never could rend this man apart.

The years that snowed upon his hair
Could never harm him anywhere.

I wish that men might think of me
Along with ships far out at sea,

Think of me in ways of weather,
Mix me and thunderheads together.

Remember me by a weather vane
Pointing to beauty and the rain.

The smallest and commonest rituals of country living
have oftenest the largest and rarest humanity in them. Boys
and girls are familiar ware, world-wide. A willow whistle,
made only in the Spring of the year when the bark comes
off easily, is a commonplace. Spring is no rare thing. But
put these commonplaces together, and you have a music
under-running all life. I have done this. And in the form of
a recipe, most familar and universal form of writing. And
I believe I have come out at the end with starry matter. As
I go through my poem, I shall stop (though it is a heinous
thing to do in a poem, as it breaks the rhythm of the words
and idea) in the interest of the science of poetry (and poetry
is one of the exactest as well as one of the oldest sciences in
the world) to show how absolutely essential each ingredient
in this recipe is.

By the way, I am not the first poet to discover that Spring
is a good season for a poem. Many older poets have anticipated me in this discovery. In the Middle Ages, indeed, all
poets assumed that Spring was the sole poetic season and
placed all their poems there. Only once did my master
Geoffrey Chaucer break the rule. He wrote one Winter-piece.

The Green Carpet

It is so lovely I wish he had tried more! It is in the *Franklin's Tale:*

> And this was, as the bokes me remembre,
> The colde frosty seson of Decembre.
> Phebus wex old, and hewed lyk latoun,
> That in his hote declinacioun
> Shoon as the burned gold with stremes brighte;
> But now in Capricorn adoun he lighte,
> Wher-as he shoon ful pale, I dar wel seyn.
> The bittre frostes, with the sleet and reyn,
> Destroyed hath the grene in every yerd.
> Janus sit by the fyr, with double berd,
> And drinketh of his bugle-horn the wyn.
> Biforn him stant braun of the tusked swyn,
> And 'Nowel' cryeth every lusty man.

Well, now, to my Spring poem:

How to Make a Willow Whistle

> You must run back through your years
> To slim boy with wide ears,

(I have to confess, at the outset, that wide ears are not absolutely essential on the boy. But I like wide ears on a boy, so I threw them in. I threw them in at the beginning, where they would do least harm. If I had put them in at the end of the stanza, it would have crippled my poem)

> Going home in homemade pants,
> Not at a run so much as a dance.
> You must have a voice as shrill
> As peepers piping under a hill.

(If your voice has changed, you cannot take part in this poem. You may fit into another, even better, poem of Spring than this, but not into this one)

> Middle Maytime it must be
> And red fringe on the maple tree.
> The schoolhouse must have woods about,

(If there weren't any woods there, you couldn't find any wood for your whistle)

> And the school must be just out,

(This is an *after*-school poem; it never could happen just before school. I doubt if anything creative could happen just before school. I know how I look, I know how I feel just at the beginning of a class. It is like a man who has just slipped on the ice and before he hits. No, this is essentially *after* school)

> And many boys

(If there weren't any other boys, there would be no poem. You must have competition here. This detail is most essential)

> and one small girl

(This is absolutely essential, I insist. There must be only *one* girl. Two girls—goodbye poem! I don't know how they do it, but two girls wrap themselves around each other and insulate themselves against the impact that must be made here)

[34]

Are going your way, and there's the curl
Of a new moon.

Don't think the moon is just thrown in. It is the most neces-
ary thing in the poem. It stands as a symbol for what comes
ext)

You are thinner
Than the moon is, aeons from dinner.

Hunger, that makes a little boy thin as the new moon, is
he most important item in my poem. And because it is the
most important, I have put it last in the list. Hunger to a
mall boy is a very tangible thing. Everything is tied in with
unger and the thin new moon. Everything in the poem is
lender—the little boy and girl, the sounds the peepers make,
he boy's ears, the maple buds. This is the fact that ties all
ogether. This poem never could happen on a full stomach.
t is an empty-stomach poem. A poem of hunger)

Take the jack-knife that has not
Lost the heat of you since the hot
Big hand of an uncle gave you it,

And you have been carrying it around in your rear pocket
ver since, and it has been pressing itself in intaglio right into
ou ever since, but you are sure it is there and you haven't lost
t)

Cut a willow branch Spring has lit,
Notch it a thumb's length from the tip,
Moisten it over on your lip,
Take your knife and tap and tap,
Turn it, turn it. When the sap

Shows everywhere, then hit the pin,
Drive the wood from its dark skin.
This is the ticklish part of it,
And it takes brains and lots of spit.
Cut a slab along one side
And slip the twig back in its hide.

Put the slot end to your lips,
And blow and blow. The girl who trips
Ahead will stop and wait for you,
And you will pay no attention to
The girl at all, but blow your soul
Out clear and high through the willow's hole.
She will walk with shining eyes,
Her swinging dress will brush your thighs,
She will hear the woods rise sweet
Up through you from your bare brown feet,
She will not mind the other boys
But drink in the willow's slender noise
And walk beside you worshipping
The mystery you are and Spring.

It is amazing what simple country things can add up to a
Milton: "Daisies pied," "the tanned haycock," "chequered
shade," a rooster strutting before his dames, the moon "stoop-
ing" through a cloud, the bee's "honeyed thigh," "the cow-
slip's velvet head," the "spruce" Spring. Such are the veriest
infants of poetry, like barefoot boys and willow whistles; but
of such is the kingdom of poetry, as of heaven.

No matter how common the days are as they come on in
the seasons, the days of a farm have a wholeness upon them,
being marked with the whole patterns from seed to harvest
which workdays in the city never can show. The sense of

continuity and sweep is there, *alpha* to *omega* in all things, the flow of the small into the vast. Even very small boys in this green world can sense the continuity and wholeness, even at a supper of homely bread-and-milk on the back doorstep:

> The boy dipped in his kitchen spoon,
> He would be a tall man soon
> Like his father, his father said,
> And go out evenings with the moon.
>
> He would marry a girl he knew
> And have a horse, or maybe two.
> The sweetpeas were like little birds
> Beside the stoop, but never flew.
>
> The morning-glory strings got tight
> Each time when it was coming night.
> His knees would not be bare at all,
> Trousers would hide them out of sight.
>
> Cows would be good to have around,
> Their bells had an evening sound,
> Milk was always cool outdoors,
> His toes were the color of the ground.
>
> A man would never want to wade
> In the pools a shower made,
> This spoonful was the last there was,
> Tomorrow he'd play house in the shade.

Strange, yet it is so; a man sees himself best when he looks at himself in small boys and colts that fit so naturally with their green background. The innocents are the essentials, as both religion and poetry have declared, of the good life. The

best stuff of poetry is the same as the good stuff of the kingdom of heaven, or whatever one wishes to call the area of
good will and stout belief. Strange yet right that animals
should preach humanity! On the green carpet of the countryside, man has always gone up in his mind by lowering himself among the gentle feeders on the grass. In his innocence
here, man has come closest to the holiest and highest. The
countrymen have dipped their hands in poems and religion
itself.

O fortunatos nimium sua si bona norint!

There are still, as there always have been, "mute inglorious
Miltons" in the barns, smelling of clover and timothy. Among
the best daily chores these innocent Miltons have the chance
to come upon the radiances of natural poems, such lights as
furnished a cradle to Christianity itself. Humble beasts are
close to the pattern of the stars.

> The satin mice creaking last Summer's grass
> Come on dry wine of miraculous clover;
> They know; their eyes sprinkle the barn with stars;
> They have no history to seal their sharp eyes over.
> The pullets on the rafters in the henhouse,
> Cockerels, whose eyes see through earth's crust
> And track the midnight sun, believe tomorrow
> Will strew incredible kernels in their dust.
> Only the farmer fumbling, cold and slow,
> With his pail and pitchfork does not know.
>
> Every last white-eared sheep in the pen turns amber
> At her trusting eyes in the lantern light,
> Remembers, without memory, such another

The Green Carpet

Frosty time and wild wings snowing the night.
The cows know, without knowledge, it once happened,
And happen again in this new barn it may;
Their eyes grow large and tremulous foreseeing
The sun like a gentle daisy in their hay.
Even the milker stroking warm teats half believes
Such things as gods could be on Christmas Eves.

He who walks green ways is always close to the road to
Damascus, to the vision that alters the chemistry and physics
of living in the twinkling of an eye. It is but a step from
kindliness and good will to the blinding revelation of a
goodness not made by man but forever there, back of the
stars, beyond the nebulae, a secret concatenation of cruelty,
splendor, and tenderness.

There is strange holiness around
Our common days on common ground.

I have heard it in the birds
Whose voices reach above all words,

Going upward, bars on bars,
Until they sound as high as stars.

I have seen it in the snake,
A flowing jewel in the brake.

It has sparkled in my eyes
In luminous breath of fireflies.

I have come upon its track
Where trilliums curled their petals back.

I have seen it flash in under
The towers of the midnight thunder.

Now in a world too crowded with citizens and blighted
by the dead will of the group, in a time of demon-like
willfulness, on an earth insane after material security only,
in a time of welfare states that would drain the very souls out
of their citizens, it is a good thing to have solitudes of the
country to turn to, where a man can still be alone and lonely
and grow sad with the natural sadness of Autumn and
evening, with Winter and old age, and the decay of hopes
and houses under the sun. Sadness is the greatest want in the
world now. And the natural world, the green, still offers this
sadness: in the fall of the leaf, the breaking of marriages and
the coming of long silences in a house, in the whitening of
hair. It is something a man needs for his growth, for his
growing tender of heart. Loneliness is another name for
poetry, as it is another name for religion. Fear, the first wisdom.

The Housing of the Lambs

It had been her blessed lot
To know the many kinds of fear,
To keep her clean and pitiful;
But one sound she would always hear.

That was when she was a child
Years ago, and it was night,
A March wind shook the window panes,
And there was snow and candle light.

From her bedroom she could hear
Her father's feet come stamping in,

The Green Carpet

Her mother's sudden gentle cry,
And then a wailing weak and thin.

She pressed the covers to her ears,
But nothing that the child could do
Could shut the terror quite away,
The cry of the baby lamb came through.

So small and far away and sad,
The tiny sound was outside all
The kindness and the world she knew
Between the shed and parlor wall.

It seemed as if the whole wide night
Was between her and the cry
Of the new-born lamb she heard—
The wind, the stars, and all the sky.

Her mother whispered tense and quick,
Her father answered low and full,
She could smell hot gin and strange
Fragrance of the singeing wool.

The thing her parents were about
Out there where the embers were
Was something sad and beautiful
That had to do with God and her.

She lost the lamb in sleep at last,
But her closed eyes were full of tears,
And that night would remain with her
Like a rainbow through the years.

The country sadness is a creative thing.
The green carpet is for dancing. In the days when small

boys choose little girls for games; when youths choose young women for wives. Green is for dancing, in the days of our youth. But the green carpet is even more the place for the "still sad music of humanity," for the airs of sorrow that bring tenderness and charity. The green poems of the folk are sad poems, more often than not. A. E. Housman is the voice of this folk-melancholy that keeps life going hopefully on, in the face of the passing of the handsome and strong ones, strong in sadness, to the generations to come. Dry hermit of a scholar, Housman never was sad for himself. He was sad for man:.

> They say my verse is sad: no wonder;
>   Its narrow measure spans
> Tears of eternity, and sorrow,
>   Not mine, but man's.

The good, green, sad songs are chiefly the songs that this most perfect of modern poets has. Dancing on the green, yes, but the dancing leads, as the stars come on, always to a finer, more creative thing—the leaving of the dancing to later girls and lads to do:

> The youth toward his fancy
>   Would turn his brow of tan,
> And Tom would pair with Nancy
>   And Dick step off with Fan;
> The girl would lift her glances
>   To his, and both be mute:
> Well went the dances
>   At evening to the flute.

The Green Carpet

Wenlock Edge was umbered,
    And bright was Abdon Burf,
And warm between them slumbered
    The smooth green miles of turf;
Until from grass and clover
    The upshot beam would fade,
And England over
    Advanced the lofty shade.

The lofty shade advances,
    I fetch my flute and play:
Come, lads, and learn the dances
    And praise the tune to-day.
To-morrow, more's the pity,
    Away we both must hie,
To air the ditty,
    And to earth I.

In the towns and cities of the world, lovely, lively things glow and fail and fall. They are replaced by others. But other new things. The cult of novelty is the history of man in his towns. All must be new under the sun. Only in the country do things dare to remain old and enduring. Only the country colors, blue of the sky, yellow of dandelions, green of the leaves, keep on unfaded. Ten thousand times ten thousand suns cannot wear their hues out. And youth and hope, love, the red beat of the heart are all of this same order of creation as these country cousins of theirs. Trite and common, ages old; yet in the setting of green they do not appear so; they appear as sharp and moist and new as this moment's rainbow trailing its watery fire on that tangle of hour-old briar roses as this same rainbow trailed its iridescent colors in Noah's water-weary eyes. There is no beginning, no middle, no end to natural goodness. Time troubles it not. Death feeds life, life shines and declines into death, and is reborn on the green wings of next moment's mayfly, with a day of life before him. There is no end to the ribbon of insistent tenderness and courage that binds all the green years past to the green years to come. There is no end to the springing of new trees from the old and dead. Disaster and decay are flowered over by new blossoms. Disaster brings towered cities to the dust; but disasters in the green world are the blossoms of tomorrow. Water passes to the sun, falls to the earth in dews and rains, runs to the sea, and is drawn up in the golden mists again, and the circle is never done, though it is perfect and whole in the doing. Men and women who live in this circling dance of renewing life grow naturally into handsome men and women. Lucy is no myth. Lucy is the truth:

> "She shall be sportive as the fawn
> That wild with glee across the lawn
>   Or up the mountain springs;
> And hers shall be the breathing balm,
> And hers the silence and the calm
>   Of mute insensate things.
>
> "The stars of midnight shall be dear
> To her; and she shall lean her ear
>   In many a secret place
> Where rivulets dance their wayward round,
> And beauty born of murmuring sound
>   Shall pass into her face."

The Green Carpet

The poems of the country come on endlessly and young.
Years and cities cannot change them. They flow in inevitable
continuity and community.

There Will Be Bread and Love

I, Tristram, since my life roots deep in pain
Like ancient Tristram's, have the right again
To say the final things, and say them plain,
Being a poet. And I say them now.

I say you people have the right to trust
In certain things that will be, when our wars
Are over, or within them, if they last:
Water, I say, is one. There will always be
Blue water through the branches of some tree
And water high up as a wall behind some houses
And white sails going up, water by roads,
And maybe beasts will drink it under their loads,
Water in forests, and thin deer will drink it,
Or birds will dip it up drop after drop
Too feverishly beautiful to stop,
Lifting bright beaks to thank whoever made it.
I say there will be hills, and trees will climb them
Gripping the rock with strong and knowing roots,
There will be hills with white clouds, and some fruits.
There will be cows to milk because it is evening
And they were lately big and bland with young,
New calves will totter under a rough tongue,
There will be milk for lambs and colts and others,
There will be fires lit and some songs sung.
Maybe the shapes of houses, cities, classes,
Vehicles, and laws will somewhat change,
But tools will not, and mothers leaning to babies,

[45]

On the Green Carpet

Giving the breast to them, will never seem strange.
No man's hand will ever be too bony,
Too cold from killing his own kind to take
A small son's hand in it and warm its fingers,
And when a strong man dies, some hearts will ache.
Always there will be some shapes like plows
Opening up furrows, sons got, hay in mows.
I do not think we ever shall finish with trees
Or have enough of honey, lambs, or bees.
I think a brother will be harder, tenderer
On a brother than on other men
And, being so, maybe will have wisdom
To be a brother to some nine or ten
Men who have a different man for father.
I think, too, that young men always will rather
Be with girls than their own kind in May.
There will be bread and love. These things, I say.

This is that green carpet, the place where the poet may
find his best true-love, the true-love who will never age or
alter. Here is the carpet of man's salvation.

The Green Carpet

On the green carpet here we stand,
Take your true-love by the hand,
Hold her now forever fast,
Only on green will sweet love last.

Only here where brave bright birds
Sing their love songs without words,
Where years outwit old mortal time
Will love forever keep her prime.

All other greens and blues will fade
Save on this carpet the sun has laid,

The Green Carpet

Save this green that shapes the deer,
The blue on bluebirds year by year.

Time will fade the bluest eyes
But not the fast blue of the skies,
Red cities will fade past reach of grief,
But not the bluebird, not the leaf.

Golden girls and bronze boys gray,
But not blue April, emerald May.
Let us carve our hearts in the beech
And grow out of ruin's reddened reach.

So shall we spring from Winter snows
At each resurrection of the rose,
Reborn in all green gracious things
Our hearts will widen to all Springs.

Here on the green, love, we join hand
With tens of thousand years of tanned
Sons of the sun, all the wheat's daughters
In all green pastures, by all still waters.

Safe now with farmers, thrushes, rams,
With snow of everlasting lambs
We stand in the rainbow's instant sheen
Here on eternity's own green.

II

THE SALVATION WHICH IS
THE NORTH

2. The Salvation Which Is the North

The flowers of the earth are many. As far back as poetry goes, they go. That is, of course, much farther than civilization or any of the religions still on the earth today. Flowers have always stood the poet in good stead. The man of religion, when he wanted to give people an idea of the kingdom of heaven, called their attention to the lilies of the field. Flowers are the natural companions of children. They go with the old into the grave as the last treasures of the earth, which might accompany a man into the hereafter. The time of year, the setting, as well as the shapes and fragrances of flowers, determine their worth. The small single English primroses which star the English Spring early, Shakespeare's wild daffodils,

> That come before the swallow dares, and take
> The winds of March with beauty,

outweigh the heavy roses of Summer. But of all the flowers of this world I am sure, being a New Englander, mayflowers are the most beautiful. When ice still shines in our northern woods, on a south-leaning hill where the soil is thin and the spare March sunshine is hoarded in outcropping granite, ten feet from the snow, ten feet from Winter, you can turn back the dead leaves, and there is Spring!

[53]

The ivory and coral stars of the trailing arbutus, first of all the northern flowers, shining up and sending up an aroma that must be like heaven. Heralds of slim Spring, rising from death, the flowers of resurrection!

> Under bare boughs, in ruined forests
> Where axes have laid the lovely low,
> In dead leaves shines the resurrection
> Under the skies still spitting snow.
>
> O first and fiercest of the flowers!
> Feeding on sunlight in the ledge,
> You turn white Winter into living
> Snow beside the snowdrift's edge.
>
> Your waxen stars valiant and hairy
> Fend off the frost, your pungent smells
> Wake up love, the Spring, the peepers
> Into millions of tingling bells.
>
> My father wore you to his wooing,
> My mother carried you to her grave,
> You taught me at the brink of boynood
> Loveliness is very brave.

Rare, sparse blossoms that are like the sparing New England emotions themselves, mayflowers keep the green of the green carpet an evergreen under the snow. They are the salvation that links year to year. These mayflowers will serve me as my motif in this chapter. They blossom when the year is all gray death, when the maples are but lines of etching on the Winter moon, before the wild geese bring Spring back in living arrows to our north. These flowers have always meant most to New England. They mean the opening of the door into the green half of the year. They are the metonymy of our natural poetry, our hard-won Proserpine, the synecdoche of our fertility, the rainbow after our Winter storms. They stand for the North, the greenest corner of our planet's green carpet because it is not always green but for six of our months must be gray and sere.

The poetry of the Near East, in our *Bible,* is magnificent poetry because its blossoms are hard-won from aridity. There is the rose of Sharon, the lily of the valley, infrequent flowers in an arid land, flowers of the oasis, the green of the few cedars of Lebanon. The natural poetry of the Mediterranean is a splendid one, too. It has infinite richness and variety. Green girls turning into laurel trees, nymphs running into fountains, hyacinths made from exclamations of grief, violets that weave a crown for Athena, the soul borrowing the wings of the butterfly, goats that are half men, men half thundering horses, kings with kingdoms of oxen and towers of bullocks, goddesses that are sheaves of the wheat, gods that are the very waves of the sea. Never was there a more constant and eloquent crasis of man with the green carpet, the leaves of his vines, the flocks of his sheep. Never more marriages of handsome trees and men, analogies of men's oaken strength and endurance, metaphors of fragrant girls and roses. In metres more magical and musical than ours, more like the running stream and the air, in polysyllabic words that are figures of speech and modulated metaphors, in pictures like bronze or marble, the Greek and Latin poets have commemorated this green carpet which underlies all our prosperity and our hope of immortality. Sappho sings the perfect song of the loveliest apple of all, the one missed by the pickers, hung like a topaz on the topmost twig of the tree. Sappho writes the seed-song of all songs of evening:

> Thou Eve bringest home once more
> All creatures to their rest,
> All that the light of day
> Scattered and led away,
> Thou bringest the lamb,
> The kid to its dam,
> The child to mother's breast.

One would think, surely, that the green carpet of our welfare could never be so well celebrated again as by these ancient ancestors of ours on the wine-dark Mediterranean Sea, in the natural pastorals of Sicily and the Aegean islands, on the chromo-like steeps of Italy and Gaul and Spain. Horace inherits the Greek sureness and purity of metaphor, the Greek economy of saying the loveliest in the simplest way. There could not be another such lyric so pure bronze or gold. Horace, tired of his city, celebrates the everlasting green of his Sabine countryside, the olives and pines that shine through Winter snows, the blue of Soracte, the fountains that bubble out running life from under limestone and marble. The seasons come and go in him; but even in Winter there are roses and leaves. He sees the green carpet's immortality in the return of the Mediterranean Spring:

> *Diffugere nives, redeunt iam gramina campis*
> *Arboribusque comae;*
> *Mutat terra vices et decrescentia ripas*
> *Flumina praetereunt.*

Surely this green carpet's songs could never be bettered.

Yet bettered they have been, in a hundred poets of the North of Europe, the lands which were dark death and forests and mystery and terror to the Greek and the Roman, *Ultimae Thules* of ice and snow and savage men. And the Classical nature songs have been bettered around the earth, in the North Temperate and South Temperate zones, wherever the sons of the cold North have spread themselves in colonies. Out of barbarian lands, forests and fens, and sea-headlands seen only now and then in the sun, in tongues that would fall uncouthly on Greek and Roman ears, a lovelier and more powerful poetry by far than the Mediterranean has sprung. In German and English, in French and Scandinavian languages new poems of the green carpet have come, with deeper tones and more moving metaphor and metonymy.

For this North in our ancestry, this North Temperate geography in our bones and our blood would have its say. And its say has produced the most eloquent lyric poetry the world knows. For its say is sadness, and its hopes are greener for the brevity of the beauty we have been a part of, in lands of long twilights, in lands of long Winters and short Summers, in lands of deeper shadows, darker storms, dim fogs, and icy death, lands where darkness *is* death, where the seas sound more like forever and the paths of men go up and down the wicked waves. Our forests where all leaves fall grew into our marrow; our roses so bitterly brief in our quick Summer got into the red of our blood; our days when the sun shines for only a moment, like a vista into eternity, got into our minds; our long-drawn-out evenings grew into our souls. The elemental sadness of deep Autumns, of long twilights, of annual ruins of ice and snow, the storm, the dark, the cold, the fierce fertility of the green half of our year became ourselves, and they became our poems.

It was inevitable that we should come to see human life in the flight of a small sparrow out of the Winter's night, through the lighted hall, away into another unknown of the dark and cold. It was inevitable that the elegy which is the coming of the slow evening should shape our elegies in country churchyards and on country greens for dancing. It was natural that men should come to see themselves in the fall of the leaf, the end of their vigors and names and works under the obliterations of storm and snow. It was a right and good thing for men to think of life as essentially sad, youth very brief, like the quick flowers of the North, to think of solitude and loneliness as the sinews of strong men, to believe that man was a cousin to brief Summer. This northern sadness, grounded in our geography, rooted in our weather, became the very makings of a man. The annually ruined rose could survive in its roots; so in his sons, in other lifetimes, in other tough enduring strengths, could he. Death was at his elbow in every creeping twilight, under every cloud, behind every wave; yet he always would come out again, if only briefly, if only in his courageous sons, into the brief suns of happiness. The knowledge of his sad estate made him strong. Death at his elbow made him more alive; inertia by his side made quicksilver of him. It was good for a man to know he moved in metaphor, to know he lived in poetry. Kings could think of Winters as the days of their dethronements and disasters, and of Summers as their return to power,

The Salvation Which Is the North

Now is the Winter of our discontent
Made glorious Summer by this sun of York!

The bitter, hard weather, and the brief beautiful, could come to be more important than love itself. The boughs stripped of leaves and birds could become more moving than a lost lady herself. For the Dark Lady is not so lovely as the poetry of the English seasons in Shakespeare. The English weather and geography shine through the vague particular passion, lost now in oblivion, and keep these sonnets present and alive.

These are the axioms of our North, and axioms built into our very sense of the mortal and the beautiful: Where the rose is brief, the rose will be cherished the more; where sunshine is sparse, sunlight will be more loved; where the day is short, day is more precious and clung to more passionately; where the Summer is so brief and the Winter so long, Summer will be life's breath itself and Winter another word for death.

We have our Horace of the North, and he through the growing centuries of the years outshines and outsings the Roman. Herrick, unwilling singer of English Devonshire, taking direct from Horace, or through "Saint Ben" Jonson, all the essential themes of the Latin poet, the brevity of youth, *carpe diem,* the joys of the simple rustic living, betters them, deepens them, makes them into psalms of life. For Herrick's North is on his side, the briefer flowers of Devon, the shorter Summer, the inevitable fall of all the leaves. The sadness of quick decay makes his "Gather ye rosebuds while ye may" more poignant and more pitiful. The likeness of English girls to the English Spring makes a song of particulars into a hymn for all humanity, his pretty particulars become solemn universals for us all:

> Fair daffodils, we weep to see
>   You haste away so soon;
> As yet the early-rising sun
>   Has not attained his noon.
>   Stay, stay,
>   Until the hasting day
>   Has run
>   But to the even-song;
> And, having prayed together, we
>   Will go with you along.
>
> We have short time to stay as you,
>   We have as short a Spring;
> As quick a growth to meet decay,
>   As you, or any thing.
>   We die,
>   As your hours do, and dry
>   Away,
>   Like to the Summer's rain;
> Or as the pearls of morning's dew,
>   Ne'er to be found again.

Always Herrick performs this miracle, which is, it may well be, the secret strength of all English poetry: he makes small particulars vast universals, blue violets into azure laws. Robert Herrick goes, single, to wake up one local Corinna to prepare herself for a single English Maytime jubilation; he starts with a slender lonely flute; and as he moves in his slender song, he wakes up gradually a world-wide orchestra, woodwinds, strings, and trumpets. All girls, all youths, all life, all times hear his insistent and fierce whisper to make the most of joy while it lasts. He wakes up all the world. What began as a small seventeenth-century lyric becomes a magnificent major poem for all the earth. Herrick's singles become multitudes. Brittle, temporary pleasures become the breath in the ribs at last. Small persuasions become fierce mandates to mankind:

> Come, let us go, while we are in our prime,
> And take the harmless folly of our time.
>> We shall grow old apace and die
>> Before we know our liberty.
>> Our life is short, and our days run
>> As fast away as does the sun;
> And as a vapor or a drop of rain,
> Once lost, can ne'er be found again:
>> So when or you or I are made
>> A fable, song, or fleeting shade,
>> All love, all liking, all delight
>> Lies drowned with us in endless night.
> Then while time serves, and we are but decaying,
> Come, my Corinna, come, let's go a-Maying.

And the English poet has his North to thank for this particular and peculiar and passionate deepening of his song. Herrick has the northern year, the smaller, quicker-blooming, more fragile violets and hawthorn flowers of the North on his side. So, in coming north, a Roman poet becomes more bronze than his bronze Latin. Horace goes out wider to a wider world. The sadness of our Summer flowers makes his Epicureanism a law of life.

[61]

So it is, too, with our modern Herrick, A. E. Housman. In an awkward monosyllabic language, with less of the suavity and civilization which are Latin and Horace, the Worcestershire poet, who has made Shropshire more universal than Horace's Sabine farm, turns Horace's argument for making the most of time into a more splendid hymn of life because he has the North in him. His snows of the cherry are close to the snow from which they suddenly spring around Eastertide,

> Loveliest of trees, the cherry now
> Is hung with bloom along the bough,
> And stands about the woodland ride
> Wearing white for Eastertide.
>
> . . . .
>
> About the woodlands I will go
> To see the cherry hung with snow.

Housman's rose-lipt girls are handsomer than Horace's girls, for the northern roses have not so long to last; they belong to a clime where roses are quicker to fade. The metaphor of decay is a North Temperate Zone fact. Our *carpe diems* are written into our calendars; our analogies are frosts and facts, not the philosophical abstracts of Mediterranean lands. Housman's Spring is closer to cold, Winter, closer to the facts of man's quick and inevitable decay; hence his theme of youth is more convincing. Housman did not write his own passionate poetry, but called in a thousand years of young English yeomen to write his poetry for him. It has behind it, in language as in analogy, the long experience of northern man, mindful of the ruins of his Summers in his Winters, the saddening ruins of ten thousand bright days in ten thousand twilights. Northern man is Uricons heaped on Uricons. The ruins of this year's leaves he has watched over many centuries; he has seen the bright banners of Summer flying and torn to death time out of mind:

> With the great gale we journey
>   That breathes from gardens thinned,
> Borne in the drift of blossoms
>   Whose petals throng the wind;
>
> Buoyed on the heaven-heard whisper
>   Of dancing leaflets whirled
> From all the woods that Autumn
>   Bereaves in all the world.

Ruins are no news to this northern man. He has seen the downfall not only of a Roman Empire but the ruins of thousands on thousands of his days and years. He comes by his sadness naturally, through his long survival in sadness. The storms in him are even older than the storms of a Roman soldier; for he lives in a northern place where gales are the rule:

> Then, 'twas before my time, the Roman
>   At yonder heaving hill would stare:
> The blood that warms an English yeoman,
>   The thoughts that hurt him, they were there.
>
> There, like the wind through woods in riot,
>   Through him the gale of life blew high;
> The tree of man was never quiet:
>   Then 'twas the Roman, now 'tis I.

[63]

The gale, it plies the saplings double,
  It blows so hard, 'twill soon be gone:
To-day the Roman and his trouble
  Are ashes under Uricon.

The salvation which is the North is sadness. Sadness learned from the elements of elegy in our twilights, our storms, our Autumns, our annual Winter extinctions of life in the dark half of the circle of our year. Melancholy, for our English poets, has been their best strength. We have learned from our sorrowful days to grow tender and courageous, in the face of ruin.

It has been so as far back as our poetry goes, for over twelve hundred years. The main eloquence of the Anglo-Saxon poetry is melancholy. Here is a poetry rooted in sorrow. And that sorrow comes from the long shadow of our long twilights and from the dark days in our northern calendar, the quick decay of our Summers, the brevity of nature's flourishing, so like that of man's. The themes of happiness are few and momentary. The sad themes many and constant. The strong man decays as his day, as his sunlight, as his Summer. The goddess behind the new Christian God is the faceless Wyrd, born of the mists and the inclement meteorology of the cold high shoulders of the earth; the fact of hard weather is behind that hard goddess, as the facts of hard weather and frost are behind the thunderings of cousinly Thor and the final Twilight of the Gods when snow and decay have their stern way at last for good and all. Like man, like Summer; like twilight, like life; and the end is elegy. The snowing of seagulls and the kiss of the hail are in our marrow and our poetry:

[64]

The hail flew in showers about me; and there I heard only
The roar of the sea, ice-cold waves, and the song of the swan;
For pastime the gannets' cry served me; the kittiwakes'
   chatter
For laughter of men; and for mead-drink the call of the sea-
   mews.
When storms on the rocky cliffs beat, then the terns, icy-
   feathered,
Made answer; full oft the sea-eagle forbodingly screamed. . . .
How weary I oft had to tarry upon the seaway!
The shadows of night became darker, it snowed from the
   north.

No wonder light is precious to the Anglo-Saxon. The sun
is God's blessed candle. The faint northern sunlight coming
thinly over the high edge of the earth is his joy. This and the
brief light and warmth of the mead-hall, the gathering of a
few friends around a fire, joy of the harp—indoors gladness.
For the outdoors is a place of woe and defeat, danger and
sorrow and decay. The evil dark, the creeping deaths of twilight are the chief dwellers there. Goodness goes out of the
world with the fading of the light:

>   Light thickens; and the crow
> Makes wing to the rooky wood:
> Good things of day begin to droop and drowse;
> Whiles night's black agents to their preys do rouse.

This, one has to remind himself, is Elizabethan poetry, not a
passage from *Beowulf.* The Anglo-Saxon concept of the dark
is so enduring it casts a shadow on even the Renaissance English mind. *Macbeth,* with the three Weird Sisters directing it

from the mists, is a play pitched in the key of the North, in the key of half-lights of twilight. Banquo "walked too late," when the west had only faint glimmers of day. It was night that was the murderer of Duncan. The villain of *Macbeth* is the meteorology of the North, and its hero is ruined by corruption that creeps upon him from the sinister dark. A chief, a king against his dark weather. And the weather wins.

Around the zone of the short days and the long twilight and nights, the circle of sad Autumn and gloomy Winter, the poetry of our race, rooted in the weather, has girdled the globe. In my part of America, long Winters, short Springs, the melancholy of the sea, the uncertainty of weather, storms, the suddenness and brevity of life are more telling features of the carpet which is green than even in the more northern but more clement England, Germany, and Scandinavia. So we take courage from our natural situation and grow stronger for sadness, just as our Anglo-Saxon ancestors did from theirs. We have learned to live with the mournful and the low sun.

Our fogs that mean peril to our boats and our coast live are, as they were a thousand years ago, the makings of men. They come upon us, not like the kittens of Lake Michigan which my friend Carl Sandburg celebrates in his poem, but like parts of a floating universe. They are portions of that Lost Atlantis of death, that dark continent moored forever off our shores, eight hundred miles wide in Winter, fifteen hundred miles wide in Summer, which, on any Summer's day, without a word of warning, save of melancholy lighthouse horn, may come unmoored and drift in upon us, erasing half of our world:

The Fog

He knew how Roman legions looked, for he
Had seen the Maine coast fogs march in from sea
For many years now, in the August days.
They came in mighty columns up the bays,
Tawny and gray and silver in the sun;
They trampled out the seaports one by one,
The islands and the woods, with their high hosts,
And pushed the world back inland from the coasts.

This little house was lost, these hills and dells,
Cows in a pasture faded into bells,
The world around a man closed in and in
Till nowhere was ten paces from his chin.
A man drew up and halted with a start
To be so close to his own beating heart
And left so to himself and wholly blind
To everything but what was in his mind.

This was the peril and the comfort, too,
A man who lived in such a region knew;
On any Summer's day, within an hour,
He might be blind and naked to a power
So vast, it might have come from stars unmade,
Undreamt of, even, making him afraid,
So mightier than the night that he could guess
How life was but a name for loneliness.

As I say in my poem, such a universe of peril, by shutting a
man away from men, by shutting a man up in himself, in
solitary being, can make him more in love with the solitude
which is life. Being alone, he learns to be strong.
The loneliness of our thousands of islands back home can

do for us what the fog does for us on the mainland. It is an easy analogue to every man's being an island, alone in this universe of ours, where friends and neighbors and children are the passing boats, hailing us for a moment or two from the mists; silence and solitude are our only perpetual neighbors. These islands are our lonely little continents, each with its miniature mountains, its small harbors, its wildernesses of spruce and cedar and fir, each neighbor only to God, with one grassy green glade often set in its forest almost untouched by man, where shy deer walk as they walked in the morning of the world, heads up and unafraid, sure of the endurance of the wild to the end, sure of the goodness of the green carpet from which they came and into which they will return as bones to feed grass for younger deer, inheritors of this earth of theirs.

We of the North have twilight still on our side, too, and on the side of poetry, the living and the written. Not only is there sadness in this long-drawn-out debate between the light and dark; there is benediction and recreation also. Our elegy of twilight is also an ode to deep peace. The slow endings to our northern days, our long, tender sunsets, the miracle of the renewal of light in the afterglows of Quebec and Maine are such easy and natural poems that the most ordinary mind, the most practical man takes part in them and knows them for the poems they are without recourse to poetry at all. No man but is a poet for a time at the time when evening comes on and trails over the world her "gradual dusky veil."

The sun rolls into the spruce forests, into the mountain. The high wings of its departure lean up high and fiery against the sky, the light of them is reflected on the easter

[68]

clouds. Thrushes wall the world with flutes. Gulls swim the sunset with glory on their wings. It gets darker and lighter. The sunset's wings burn brighter. The strange mystery of a clearer light begins to wash the world. The diffused evening glow brings houses miles away close to one. Trees stand out clearer than at noon. Crickets begin their night-long prayers. The stillness becomes world-wide. Voices miles away come near. Eternities pass. Children play long games on the edge of dark, blond with the light washing all things. People talk long talks at their gates. Lovers go hand in hand long hours and say nothing. Only after ages, it seems, a few windows come out with lights, a few stars appear at the top of the sky. So, in Summer, the long poem, the three-hour-long poem of twilight unfolds over the green carpet where lambs begin at last to bleat for their mothers and think of going home.

Our fine Summer days are few, they are lovelier for being built on the law of the brevity of beauty; but they linger on in the evenings till one begins to believe they are going to last forever, and they seem plans for eternity.

I never realized the eloquence and pathos in Homer's formula for the close of the Mediterranean day, "then the sun set, and all the ways grew dark," until I visited the Mediterranean. I never knew how poor that sea was, and how poor other southern places, until I lived in the South. I knew, every day, something was lacking in this Alabama, this Florida, this Texas; but I could never put my finger on it. Then suddenly, one evening, it came full home to me. There was no twilight. The sun set, and then immediately it was night and all the stars. Coleridge put it aptly: "No twilight within the courts of the Sun." How these southern sisters of

[69]

ours in these United States have ever bred poets I cannot but wonder. With no twilights to turn their faces handsome in a common world around them, no twilights to transfigure their neighbors' faces and fences and make caskets of jewels of common trees and twigs, houses and harbors:

The South Has No Twilight

The South lacks an essential thing
When all its mocking-birds are done:
The tender, tremulous, long and sad
Farewell to the departing sun.

Night comes all at once with stars
And leaves no room for the shy wings
Of swallows on the dusk, bird flutes
That play songs of the tears of things.

There is no half a lifetime here
Of lovely loneliness coming on
Ahead of night across the hills
Before the sunset glow is gone.

I think of little northern hills
Full of deep light where cows come in
From fields where shadows reach out long,
Each cow with music under her chin.

And half the world away a thrush
Sings beside the glooming sea
As if there were before his sleep
Half of all eternity.

Voices of farmers and fishermen
Linger on the quieted air,

And only after lamps are lit
The evening star is burning there.

There is time for slender boys
With blonder hair than in the day
To play long games, for men to love
Before dark puts the world away.

I know now why Horace and Catullus were never able to
say the tenderest words and the wisest about life, but had to
leave it to Keats and Burns and Wordsworth to say them.
They had no twilight; no time for looking back at life yet
away from life, no time when time stands still and only
loveliness lives; no rest between their days and their sudden
Mediterranean nights. They lacked the sense of sadness and
security, of emptiness and fullness, too, which only a northern Autumn twilight can bring,

> While barréd clouds bloom the soft dying day,
>   And touch the stubble-plains with rosy hue;
> Then in a wailful choir, the small gnats mourn
>   Among the river sallows, borne aloft
>   Or sinking as the light wind lives or dies;
> And full-grown lambs loud bleat from hilly bourn;
>   Hedge-crickets sing; and now with treble soft
>   The redbreast whistles from a garden-croft;
>   And gathering swallows twitter in the skies.

The songs of Spring, too, on our northern half of the green
carpet are more moving than the Spring songs in Latin and
Greek. They are pure exclamations of joy at the universal
resurrection of all things from death, from the silence and
gloom of Winter.

On the Green Carpet

Wie herrlich leuchtet
Mir die Natur!
Wie glänzt die Sonne!
Wie lacht die Flur!

Es dringen Blüten
Aus jedem Zweig
Und tausend Stimmen
Aus dem Gesträuch.

Und Freud und Wonne
Aus jeder Brust.
O Erd, o Sonne!
O Glück, o Lust!

O Lieb, o Liebe!
So golden schön,
Wie Morgenwolken
Auf jenen Höhn!

Du segnest herrlich
Das frische Feld,
Im Blütendampfe
Die volle Welt.

Spring comes to us in an instant. The wild geese give us
word:

Bare willows by the pasture bars
Are budding out with furry stars,
Though ice still locks the woods, the sun
Sets a warm large Summer one.

Not a blossom, not a bird,
Yet sudden everywhere is the word

The Salvation Which Is the North

This northern world has entered the clear
Leafy green half of the year.

The word is raucous throaty words,
And down the cold green sky slant birds,
Each with a promise in the mouth,
Each with beak full of the South.

We sing our songs the louder because we know that Springs
are over quickly in our North, that the year, like ourselves,
will soon turn white, that this blossom-white is only a few
breaths away from the snow.

'Tis Spring; come out to ramble
  The hilly brakes around,
For under thorn and bramble
  About the hollow ground
  The primroses are found.

And there's the windflower chilly
  With all the winds at play,
And there's the Lenten lily
  That has not long to stay
  And dies on Easter Day.

Our sudden Springs are shouts of things as our Autumns are
tears of things. We must make the most of this swift togetherness of lovely new lives:

Now days are days of blue new weather,
Peepers and plowmen out together.

The smallest brook begins to boil,
The farmers begin to smell of soil.

On the Green Carpet

They spill their farms off in their rooms,
Their women sweep it out with brooms.

Roosters blush along their hackles,
Henpens turn to mountains of cackles.

White clouds catch on every tree,
Lambs leap on legs without a knee.

Lambs and clouds leave tufts of wool
On everything. Rain-barrel's full.

Life runs sparkling from the eaves,
Flowers come before the leaves.

Rhodora blossoms out of bark,
The shadbush shines long after dark.

The bluets ice the fields like cakes,
Hills spill long jewels of the snakes.

Round men sow the corn in rows,
Flat men stand and scare the crows.

The crows are puzzled by white twine
And they discuss it on a pine.

The frogs have sown the pool with seeds,
And future tadpoles float in beads.

Night's peepers have so much to say
They overflow into the day.

They cannot rest for anything
But shout it over, "Spring! Spring! Spring!"

The Salvation Which Is the North

But it is on the other side of our year, when the sun is dipping lower and lower to the earth, when warmth is dying out of the northern world, when Autumn blows and the leaves fall, that we find our greatest strength. It is a strength that flows from sadness. We make our deepest poems out of the ends of things. In the old days it was the most natural thing in the world to link the end of man's glory and vigor with the death of the year and the light. The sadness of the northern year was one with man's:

Where is the horse and the rider? Where
   is the giver of gold?
Where are the seats at the banquet? Where
   are the hall-joys of old? . . .
Alas for the strength of the prince! For the
   time hath passed away,
Is hid under shadow of night as it never
   had been at all.
Behind the dear and doughty there
   standeth now a wall,
A wall mysteriously high, and with
   mysterious snake-work wrought.
The strength of spears hath doomed
   the earls and made them naught,
The weapons greedy for slaughter and she
   the mighty Wyrd.
And the storm beats on the rocks and the
   gale that maketh afraid,
The fearful storm that fetters earth,
   the Winter-bale,
When the shadow of night falls wan
   and wild is the hiss of the hail,
The wicked rush from the North,

which maketh all men quail.
   Woe-full is the earth, o'erthrown
      when the stark Wyrds say;
   Here is the passing of wealth,
      here friends are passing away,
   Men and their kinfolk pass,
      nothing and none may stay;
   And all this earth-stead here shall be
      empty and bare one day.

This is the sad song often sung by the blond-haired men in our blood, as they sat over a thousand years ago by a fire at night when the north wind and Winter roared over the house outside. This is the sad song behind *Beowulf* in spite of all some pious Christian bard setting old epics to words could do; the old final melancholy, the ancient likeness of man's story to the story of the ruined year, burns and shines through all the Christian hopefulness; the sad light of the North puts out the light and hope of the South. And these ancient men in our blood, hearing this sad song chanted to the sweep of harp-strings, found a deeper joy in it than they found in the marrowbones of their feast and the warmth of their fire. They were happiest hearing their doom, knowing they were kin to the dying day and the dying glory of the year, happiest when most sad. For these men were ourselves centuries ago, men of our North; and

   Our sweetest songs are those that tell of
      saddest thought.

The Autumn is in us deep. There are no odes to Autumn in the Mediterranean world. There are none of those elegies of the green carpet which make Shakespeare seem to us more present and powerful than Aeschylus, that tie him into our seasons and geography. Shakespeare finds his most moving analogies in russet and sober Autumn, in chill winds and leafless boughs. The death of Summer and the fall of the leaf are man's history to him; he cannot separate himself from twilight, the facts of weather and fire and decay in nature:

That time of year thou mayst in me behold
When yellow leaves, or none, or few, do hang
Upon those boughs which shake against the cold,
Bare ruin'd choirs, where late the sweet birds sang.
In me thou seest the twilight of such day
As after sunset fadeth in the west,
Which by and by black night doth take away,
Death's second self, that seals up all in rest.
In me thou seest the glowing of such fire,
That on the ashes of his youth doth lie,
As the death-bed whereon it must expire,
Consum'd with that which it was nourish'd by.
   This thou perceiv'st, which makes thy love more strong,
   To love that well which thou must leave ere long.

Northern man has been trained by long experience to look for the shadow after the brightest sunshine. His weather and his seasons have schooled him to remember the end in the beginning, the doom under the bloom. In the midst of the lustiest loveliness, we look for melancholy. In the rainbows of spray, in the profuse and prodigal peony, in the beauty of a woman's face, we find

    Joy, whose hand is ever at his lips
  Bidding adieu.

It is the northern law of life.

At the azure-and-gold high-tide of Summer, on a day like crystal in our richest month, named for the richest name among Roman Emperors, in August, suddenly, with no change one can put his finger on, one knows the end of the green half of our year has come. I am not speaking poetry. I am speaking meteorology. I am speaking Maine folk-experience. And the title of my poem is an idiom I learned from practical people who have commented on this sudden turn we take in our calendar, a turn from life to death. Suddenly, without seeing any change, we know. This knowledge has happened to thousands of people before my time, and it will go on happening to thousands after, whether they read poetry or not:

The Corner of the Year

Here, at a pin's point, Summer ends;
The independent birds turn friends
All at once, they hush and eye
The long road of the open sky.

The high and hazy gentle trees
Discover a cruel growing breeze
In their branches, the trees quiver,
The skimming swallows have left the river.

Nothing is changed, yet everything
Is poised and taut, the crickets sing
Still in the grasses, on and on,
But Summer the beautiful is gone.

Blue to the north is a sky so clear
It means the corner of the year

Has been turned, from now on all
Leaves and men face to the Fall.

Frost is but slender weeks away,
Tonight the sunset glow will stay,
Swing to the north and burn up higher
And Northern Lights wall earth with fire.

Nothing is lost yet, nothing broken,
And yet the cold blue word is spoken:
Say goodbye now to the sun,
The days of love and leaves are done.

Just as sharp as that, do we feel the presence of death in our year.

Trust the green carpet as it slopes towards the snows that are forever to have melancholy and magical warnings on the wind to tell us that green must die, and men. Among the articles of salvation in my northeastern and sea-beat corner of our continent there is a wind. It is a wind that comes to us from the sea. It has a sad sound, and we keep well because of its solemn tone. It is there in the middle of our Summers, in the sunniest of our days. Whenever the wind is southerly, as it is for nearly two-thirds of our days, that sound is there. It warns us, in the midst of life, how life must have its end. The eaves and cornices of our square white-pine houses along the coast have that low warning there around them, like an aeolian harp, sad and far away. We grow up from childhood with that sound. We grow old with it. It is built into us. It keeps us sad. And well.

My son, in his training as a naval aviator in the second world war, met this wind, which was an old friend of his—

Oh, a friend of generations of him who had lived and died by the sea!—out in the very center of our continent. When, in one stage of his training, when he was learning to fly on and off a carrier, out in Illinois, on Lake Michigan, my son used to get up about a mile high, he noticed he grew suddenly, unaccountably, homesick for Maine. He wondered why. Being an inquisitive and methodical young man, he took steps to find out. He was able to put his finger on the very reason. It was because the wind around his plane, at that height, sounded identically like the wind he had grown up with from the time he was a child at home, in the south bedroom of our coast house. That little aeolian harp I speak of was always hung there on the eaves of his room. Now, out here in the dry center of the continent, that Maine coast wind had come to be with him, to befriend him. It seemed so fine a little poem I had to put it into words. And as I groped for the words, the words found themselves and a vaster meaning than I had meant; the poem grew into a more timeless and major thing than I had dreamed of writing. It formed itself into the kind of poem that grows naturally out of our North, out of our racial heritage, out of the natural rightness and sadness of winds that have shaped our history and our souls. It is the song, not only of a present Maine home, but of a windy seaward-facing home for thousands of years, on the other side of the sea, on the other side of science, a native poem of our North:

Wind from Home

Along his plane an empty blue mile high
He heard the wind go sad and make a cry,

The Salvation Which Is the North

And in this alien heaven walled around him
He knew the wind of home had come and found him.
The wind away on his own azure coast,
That little south wind hanging like a ghost
On his room's eaves, even in fairest weather,
Had come a thousand miles. They were together.

It was the wind which has the sea inside it,
The men within his blood had learned to ride it
On cloth wings leaning white along the waves
Where some of them had found their blue deep graves.
Now he was riding it on his own kind
Of sails, with land and sea both left behind.
It was the old wind in this strange new weather,
Men in his blood and this man flew together.

He closed his eyes; and he was still a boy
Falling asleep with his bright newest toy
And hearing the wind that came in off the deep
Smoothing the waves that ran with him towards sleep;
And he was earlier boys with his blue eyes
Hearing the wind from sea that cries and cries:
In years that were and will be, now and forever,
Men and the sea and wings belong together.

This wind which blew this poem into being is well-known
to men, my kinsmen, along the Maine seashore. The men
there have a name for this wind which keeps them well,
keeps them looking alive in their boats, keeps them cheerful
believers in life and trusters in nature. They have the word
for it:

The Grieving Wind

For the wind around their houses' eaves
These people have a word, they say it "grieves."

And that is the right word for the wind out there
When days are drawing in and fields grow bare.

Yet even in the Summers on this coast
Always in broad daylight there is a ghost
At every house's corner to warn men
That death and Winter always come again.

It is a good thing for householders to know
They who sleep under wool will sleep under snow,
Come so many more of the brief nights,
And wind at last will blow out the last lights.

It may well be that wind—what man can tell?—
Is the thing that keeps coast people well.
What are ghosts for if not to do the duty
Of warning men to make the most of beauty?

Hark! the little slender grief is there!
Aeolian lyre woven of hollow air.
So say your best words, comfort your love, your friend!
There is the snow, the silence at the end.

It is a natural thing that a sound of death should make men live more eagerly and deeply. That is another law of salvation in the North.

The sound of change, the sound of the turn of the tide of green life rises to its highest eloquence later than that day I spoke of in August just now. The sharpest corner of the year is a roaring place. It falls about the time of the Autumn Equinox. Oh, I know people now, thanks to scientists who measure by machines and not by men's folk-lore and myths —which are far more infallible barometers and compasses—

declare that there is nothing to the theory of the Line Gale, that the mere crossing of the Equator by the sun going south could cause no disturbance in meteorology. But I notice that sometime around the third week in September something does happen in nature, we do have a blow that stirs things up and strips our leaves from our trees. That time is a crucial corner to our year. I recall two such September gales recently that took shingles guaranteed for a lifetime off my half-acre barn roof, to my sorrow. I recall over a score of such September storms. Let the scientists go down and tell a Yankee fisherman, whose father and grandfather and great-grandfather came home alive from the four corners of the globe by learning how to dodge late September gales, that there is nothing in this theory. Though our farmers, and some fishermen today, who have been to state universities and studied agriculture and meteorology, may no longer believe in the Line Gale in their waking hours or their brains, still they do know and do feel this enduring poem of the ends of things in their bones and their sleep. It is there. It is a persisting poem of our North.

Line Gale

Trees remember if a man forgets
When the blond father of the corn goes south
Over the Line, the gales come out of hiding
With the year's leaves and whitecaps in their mouth.

The little mice remember and are shaken
In their sage galleries of etched earth and straw,
Birds solitary throng in high nations,
Turn their beaks south before inexorable law.

[83]

On the Green Carpet

The farmer in his bed, deep in his dreaming,
Feels the sun slip to the under hemisphere,
Cries his deep cry, though he knows not he cries it,
Hail and farewell to the green half of the year.

Hail and farewell! Next morning death is the caller,
On the north sides of all things lies the frost,
And fumbling fingers at the stove and hearthstones
Kindle thin suns in place of the lovely lost.

No such sad and lovely poem has ever blown over the green earth as that which comes yearly to our North in the departure of our birds for the South. That high journey in desolation by even the most minute birds and butterflies, painted sons of Summer, when Winter looks over the edge of earth, the leaves fall, and all that is green grows gray, and death is in the air! Here, finally, is one of the commonest and highest of our natural poems of the North, one that every man with eyes can see, every man with blood in him to quicken at the solemn warning of the end to all singing. It is easy for a man to make the analogy to his own transiency in this mutable world when all is flowing away, when all goings-out are departures, all speeches are farewells. Any man can read his own history in this last poem of green Summer. Any man can take what strength he can find from seeing how he, too, faces an Autumn from which there is no return in Spring.

Pity Us All

Pity now the slender traveller,
The humming-bird on trackless air,

The Salvation Which Is the North

Going south, an inch of Summer
Over the miles of earth blown bare.

Pity, too, the silken swallows
Threading high the thunderful gales
With nothing to guide them but quicksilver
Intelligence in wings and tails.

Pity the amber civilizations
In the benumbed and silent hive
With only the glassy pinions working
To keep the jewelled hearts alive.

Think with compassion on the furry
Where they dig their homesteads deep
And feed on the Summer of their bodies
Through the long Winter of their sleep.

Pity us all who shrink and perish
Thought by thought, red Fall by Fall,
Whose youth goes on the high Autumnal
Journey and comes not back at all.

For our good health, in this our North, over this green,
good carpet of ours the winds of destruction, the gales of dying leaves, blow. We stand up to them and grow stronger for
their great blowing. For sadness does make men strong. Sadness is a fine creative thing; it teaches mercy and tenderness.
Times and people that are un-sad are perilous times and
people. Our dying year is on our side in this North; frost
and the bitter gales are our teachers.

Our salvation is in sadness, in the metonymy of man's part
in the sorrows of the calendar. Here is the salvation which is
the North.

III

THE YEOMANLY SHAKESPEARE

3. The Yeomanly Shakespeare

Shakespeare is probably the most written-about writer on earth. The books about him and his poetry add up in themselves to libraries. Shakespeare scholars have endeavored to explore every angle of his greatness. In books that are often themselves literature, as those of Coleridge and Bradley, writers have tried to map every contour of the azure Andes of this Elizabethan poet's mind. All authors sooner or later are attracted to this continental genius and desire to explain him, as all actors, late or soon, burn to play Hamlet. They feel that they are here in the presence of the very law of creativeness, almost in the light of creation itself. Here are such god-like kings, such king-like commoners, such wit and graciousness of language, such wisdom sinewed by human experience, such honey hived in the dead carcasses of dead lions, dusty old dukes and kings, such manna and quail in the deserts of life, such iron in this milk of human kindness, such milk of majesty, such breadth and height of humanity, such variety, such salt and savor, such bread, such meat, such fruit and flowers, such apprehension so like a god's! No metaphors are too sweeping for him, no metonymies too daring, no analogies too wide. Surely here is the essence of poetry, the secret of the life turned into art. So these other creators of poetry, these sharp-eyed critics of poetry will resolve the riddle of Shakespeare, and, doing so, the enigma of

[91]

the creative impulse. Defining Shakespeare will be a definition of literature.

And these many scholars and critics have taken their expert tools of learning in hand and have gone to work. They have used history to unravel the mystery of Shakespeare's greatness, have tried to show that he is the child of a sudden upsurge in a little nation, like the Greek dramatists after Marathon, after its defeating a vast one in 1588. They have endeavored to show how Shakespeare's best colors come from the bright colors of the rich Elizabethan times; his elaborate wit being all of a piece with the intricate embroideries and laces and jewel-sewn clothes of the day. Yet Shakespeare has escaped them. They have proved, to their satisfaction, that the key to Shakespeare lies in his sources and the way he coalesced and manipulated them. Still Shakespeare has eluded them. Other critics, enlisting modern psychological apparatus, have labored to establish the fact that a poet, innocent of Freud and the codes of the higher apes, has nevertheless anticipated—*prevented,* Shakespeare himself would have put it—Freud's day and stumbled upon basic pathology, neuroses, and complexes. But Shakespeare seems, for all his obsession with sexual irregularity, still healthy. Other critics have turned sleuths and used the methods of Sherlock Holmes on this mystery. They have written good detective books; but they haven't written much about Shakespeare. For all these Himalayas of books on Shakespeare, this greatest poet of ours, it may be of the world, remains a paradox still.

Shakespeare *is* a paradox. No one can deny that. Here he is, sprung of a small country village, of middle-class or lower-middle-class people, not very well acquainted with the two great kindlers of the fires of the Renaissance, the Greeks and Romans. Not well-posted in contemporary history. Not skilled in the Court, though most of his plays have the Court as a background. Totally unversed in the heated politics of his day. Not well-acquainted with London. Without many influential friends. A countryman come to one of the brightest cities that have shone on this earth. A worker in a profession not so much of letters as of bread and butter. A worker in a medium scorned by the best literary people, in plays, relegated to what would now be the city dump, on the wrong side of the river, along with bear-baiting and other cheapjack pastimes. A man not well-connected, a jack-of-all-trades, revamper of other people's plays, actor as well as playwright. A man to whom poetry was a business, whose chief ambition was to make enough money to be able to go back home and play the big toad in the small puddle, buy himself a patent of gentility and retire to the status of a comfortable burgher in a town of artisans and tradesmen, more concerned, at the last, with the fate of his second-best bedstead than with the text of *Hamlet*. Such a paradox, such a mystery, is Shakespeare.

How a poetry wide as the world could have come out of this Nazareth, how a book by a stay-at-home body could come out of a small country to go westward on the path of an English-speaking empire in the Conestoga wagons of American pioneers, to be the companion of the family skillet and frying-pan, to be read along with the *Bible* as the only reading matter in high Appalachian cabins, to become a cornerstone in the making of America, as it had become a cornerstone in the poetry of the Romantic Movement in England; how such great good could have come out of such small beginnings is enough to amaze all men. Shakespeare, the *Bible* it may be of a United States of the World to come, the only poet indeed who has attained something of the status of the *Bible,* a sort of New Testament of Man, baffles the critics still after nearly two hundred years of careful study of him. Here is wisdom, apparently, from a small man; prodigality of princes from a man of the provinces. Shakespeare remains a mystery.

Because this is so, many crackpots of literature, many antics of criticism, have found ample opportunity to obliterate Shakespeare entirely, as a man merely a myth, and give all his plays and poems to my Lord Bacon, to the Sixth (or is it the Fifth?) Earl of Oxford, or anybody else with enough Elizabethan eminence upon him, even of the third water, to account even partially for the greatness in this poetry.

To understand how ill-matched Shakespeare is with the great ones in literature, one has only to glance at two greater Elizabethans than he, one of them his friend and enemy.

Shakespeare pales into insignificance as an Elizabethan beside the rich Spenser. Edmund Spenser was a university man; he was deeply read into all the greatest books of the past. He knew all the important languages, ancient and modern; Shakespeare knew but one and a smattering of another. Spenser knew the Greeks as he knew the *Bible;* he revised Plato and renewed Aristotle; he had at his finger tips all the rainbow-like anatomies of Greek mythology. He cannot touch a day or night, he cannot touch the seasons, he can-

not touch shepherds and husbandmen without kindling in
his mind with the anthropomorphic magic of the Mediterranean ancients. Morning and evening are human beings.
Qualities are lovely or evil women.

As if this was not enough learning for any one man,
Spenser knew the Middle Ages; he alone of the Elizabethans,
with the exception of the young John Donne, hydroptically
drunk with the Church Fathers, has a respect for the dark
foliations and unearthly splendors of the mediaeval mind.
He, a Renaissance Classicist, is a mediaevalist! Spenser makes
chivalry his touchstone of character; he makes Chaucer his
Tityrus, his guide; and all his life, in homage to Chaucer as
the morning star of English poetry, deliberately cripples his
ideas and his diction with worshipful archaisms and, often
erroneous, Middle English spellings and phrasings. Alone of
the Renaissance giants, Spenser respects the ethics of denial,
the mediaeval hungers in aestheticism and asceticism. Lover
of Plato's plentitudes, he yet marches with the lean spiritual
homiletics and the flat and faded, if lovely, allegories of the
twelfth century. Anchorites and hermits go side by side with
Circe and blowzy, buxom Greek nymphs and sensual satyrs.
Running the fingers of his avid mind over every voluptuous
surface of life, like a disciplined Keats, Spenser yet preaches
stern morality of the most arid mediaeval kind. Not only
does he know all Greek fable, he knows German and Celtic
fairy lore, too. In Book III of the *Faerie Queene* he goes into
a Grimm forest among Germanic creatures and down also
into a Celtic under-water world where a Greek would
drown. Above all, this neo-mediaevalist takes as the frame-

[95]

work and fire of his masterpiece the livest tissue of story, more alive than the Homeric, the livest ever achieved by man, the Arthurian cycle of tales of etiquetted virtue and fealty to the aristocratic religion of the Germanic man on horseback. His heroes move to a music that would be all Greek to the Greek Homer.

And as though all this were insufficient, this Elizabethan poet knows the regal Renaissance, Ariosto, Tasso, and the rest, the new ethics of abundance, the opulence of opportunity, the unlimited liberality, the *copia* of man's god-like power to assume the status of God himself. And in order that no wealth of civilization be wanting, doesn't Spenser have as his life-long ideal for his English verses the *sense of state* which is Virgil's *Aeniad?* His poetry is civics; his Gloriana shall be Augustus; England's empire of the mythical Arthur is the true and logical successor of the Roman *imperium.* Spenser will write a great poetry of a great and greatly growing Britain. He is a poet not merely of men but of the state, the city, the commonwealth of mankind. Prophetically he foretells the British Empire through the Kingdom of Camelot.

There is still more. Spenser knew statecraft; he was secretary to it; he was secretary to Justice, who happened to be Lord Grey, Sir Artegáll; and, though she often neglected him for her Sidneys and Leicesters and Raleighs and Essexes, Spenser, to his death, was amanuensis to Elizabeth, Defender of the Faith, Queen of the new Republic of the Protestant North. This poet sat at the center of the new English ambitions in politics; he was of the state, stately. He sat at England's heart. For his service to the state, Spenser was willing and glad to disfigure, for us, his cloth of gold with dark hate of the older Church, whose mediaeval virtues and splendors and visions he worshipped.

Not only all this, but Spenser from his youth knew the lords and ladies of his commonwealth personally. He knew and loved above all men that slim Puritan and pattern of chivalry, Sidney; he knew that stout Puritan and pattern of the sensuous Renaissance, Leicester; he was a close friend to that man of the world, who added new worlds to England's acres, soldier and sailor and chemist and courtier, the "Shepherd of the Ocean," Sir Walter Raleigh; he lived with Lord Grey; he worked for other bigwigs; he knew and adored, if distantly, that shining Britomart, that warrior lady, that splendid Amazon, that white mediaeval virgin proof against all spears, who runs like a bright strand of dream through all the *Faerie Queene,* whose source is the Tudor Queen who looked her best on horseback reviewing her troops and her fleets, reviewing her lovers—Gloriana, Elizabeth, "Great Lady of the greatest isle." Spenser knew lords and earls and monarchs as one would know cousins.

And last, yet most notable, Spenser knew the greatness of his calling. He knew he was writing great poetry. Long before, as a young man new to letters, he had debated with himself, in October of the *Shepherd's Calendar,* as two different shepherds, the issue between the pleasant private lyric and the stern state poetic; and he had chosen the highroad of the grave and stately poetry from which, for him, there could be no turning back. Spenser knew he was creating literature, as Shakespeare knew only he was doing successful plays; Spenser knew he was writing great literature, as Shakespeare

[97]

knew only that he was making a living in a lively new, if often greatly scorned, medium.

Shakespeare, to Spenser, is a little hill to a venerable mountain. He is a pygmy to this giant who has all the ancient languages and cultures at his command. What hope has a man with no codes of mediaeval chivalry built into his bones, with no codes of Plato and Aristotle as parts of his bright brain, to stand up to this giant of a poet who is heir of the ages? Shakespeare, who writes so often of kings and queens, knows none. Spenser knows mighty leaders and princes of the state. Shakespeare, unschooled in statecraft, writes of the princely as a private observer; Spenser, as a confidant and friend. The Middle Ages, in their philosophy and aesthetic, are dead matter to Shakespeare, pure pageantry and story-bookish chronicle; they are an astoundingly live history and culture to Spenser. Shakespeare gets his Greek mythology from the handy handbook or the superficial Ovid; his Roman history and biography secondhand, from translation; Spenser is a liver in and a lover of the very essences of the Greek spirit and the Roman statecraft. Shakespeare's history is chronicle; Spenser's is culture and a matter alive.

The style of Spenser's *Faerie Queene* beside Shakespeare's plays is like a rich brocade with every inch of it involved foliations of splendor beside a bright, but often homespun and plain, cloth. It is a flower garden of man's imagination in several cycles of culture, flowers of art, against the marigold meadow of the man of Stratford. History against a May-time field.

But there is an even greater contrast in Shakespeare's own day. Beside his friend and fellow playwright-actor, Ben Jonson, Shakespeare is as an unbreeched boy to an adult in doublet and hose. Ben Jonson, sprung from lower-than-middle-class men, was nevertheless a man schooled brilliantly in the Classics, and a complete citizen, not only of his brilliant London, but of all earth's great towns anywhere. Polish, principles, urbanity—they are other names for Ben. He was built of the severe and central best of the past, selected disciplines, an aristocrat in all his ideas. Shakespeare, to Ben Jonson, is a "sylvanist," a rustic.

First, Ben Jonson, unlike Shakespeare, was a critic, both of life and letters. He was the first real critic in our language; his *Discoveries Made upon Men and Matter* forms our first extended survey of the poet's art. Aristotle and Horace are his familiars. Jonson did not write for the amusement or betterment of Englishmen; he wrote for Europe; he wrote for mankind at large. He and Bacon are the first English authors who are Europeans before they are Englishmen.

Ben Jonson, Poet Laureate of England, is more. Not only is he the creator of a lyric so spare, so sparse, so brief, so economical, so crystal-clear that it stands up to the best of Horace and Martial and remains the standard of the best in lyricism to this day; he is also the first real Classicist in Europe. The great seventeenth-century Frenchmen follow him in the discovery of the true nature of Greek and Latin writing. Jonson was the first to discover that, contrary to the conception of all the Renaissance Italians and Spenser, the Classical writing is not rich, but spare, athletic, simple, straightforward. Jonson is our first lean writer; his terseness is Mediterranean. He turns his back on the rich embroiderings of the Renaissance, the use of Greek and Roman writers as gold mines for ornamentation; he restores their straight almost poverty-stricken, line. To write with simplicity, to write with restraint is to write Romanly and like the Greeks. Jonson introduces into Europe the *aurea mediocritas* of Horace, the μηδὲν ἄγαν of the Greeks. Jonson's statement of emotion is brief, declarative, as Shakespeare's is exclamatory and richly repetitious. Ben Jonson is the first of the Neo Classicists, the real learners from Rome and Athens.

Coming more closely home to Shakespeare, it may come as a shock to some critics of Shakespeare, and historians of the drama, to discover that Jonson is a milestone in the history of drama, where Shakespeare is not. Shakespeare's plays great as they are as poetry, are not great developments in the world's drama. Jonson's comedy is immensely significant. Shakespeare derives from the New Comedy of the Greeks from Menander, through Plautus and Terence, the Classical ideal of the play as diversion and entertainment. *A Midsummer Night's Dream* and *As You Like It* are picnics, vacations from life. Jonson harks back to sterner Aristophanes and his ideal of comedy as a corrective. The *Alchemist* and *Volpone* are no picnics; they are essays on the manners of man. Jonson's comedy of humours is an improvement on the Aristophanic comedy as satire; it is more Classical than the Classics; it is a study in the pathology of excess and obsession. This comedy of Jonson's is enormously influential, as Shakespeare's comedies are not, on the history of English play making; from his grave in the Poets' Corner of Westminster Master Ben, revolutionist Ben, dictates to all later English comedy; to Etherege and Shadwell, Congreve, Van Brugh Farquahar, to eighteenth-century Sheridan and Goldsmith to modern Wilde and Shaw. Jonson, unlike Shakespeare, is a milestone in literary evolution.

What is more, Ben Jonson was a complete man of his place, and his place was an European capital. Unlike Shakespeare's, Jonson's plays are full of the peculiar color of his "brave" time. They tell us what Londoners wore, what they ate, the prices they paid for things, the topics they talked and thought most about, the fashions they followed, the news of the day, even down to the oaths and colloquialisms they used; they are a projection of the genius and spirit of an era, of the nervous designs of the age of the Stuarts; they are more: they are a summary of a universal urban approach to life, of the city man's *mores*. Shakespeare, to Jonson, seems like a provincial person, a rustic again.

And, finally, Ben Jonson, Master of the Revels of the Jacobean world, collaborator in masques with Inigo Jones and Lawes, teacher and patron saint of all the Cavalier wits, the wittiest of them all himself, was in the thick of everything in his city and times. He was a friend of the king and an ornament and fixture at the Court; he knew everybody, he quarreled and made up with everybody, ate, drank, and crossed wits with all, with Shakespeare and other actor-playwrights; he was the life of all parties, literary and convivial. Ben Jonson founded a school of lyric poetry, and he left his name indelibly on his time, imprinted his habit of disciplined writing and living on an era, and left his name on half a century, the Age of Jonson. There is no Age of Shakespeare; there is no School.

Ben Jonson is as careful of his literary work as Shakespeare is careless. He published his own folio, in 1616. He knew he was writing great writing. Like Spenser, and few others in this uncertain world, he was conscious of his own great place in letters. An European, not merely an Englishman, he saw himself safely established among the literary elite of the ages; and he went to his grave in Westminster, just before his country split into two halves in the Civil War, like a king. Such a man was Ben Jonson, apprentice to a bricklayer, soldier, brawler, revolutionist, duelist, actor, play-maker, literary lion worshipped by a score of brilliant younger men, many of them born with silver and even golden spoons in their mouths. A friend and knower of kings, he wrote about London middle-class citizens; a city man first and last, he wrote of the city virtues of shrewdness, moderation, and good taste for citizens of the world in all ages.

What has Shakespeare, a drifter into literature from the bucolic hinterlands, poorly schooled in the great learning of Athens and Rome, with no sense of the greatness of poetry in him, what has such a man to offer as resources comparable to Jonson's and Spenser's? He knew little history and no kings; he knew only a handful of influential citizens. He left little or no impact on his surroundings or society. He founded no school of comedy. He created no cult of letters. The vast political changes of this time passed him by. An outsider in the city, an outsider in the Court, he wrote his lines, took his modest wages, and departed home, content to be buried in his parish church, without an inkling of the acclaim that one day would come to him, never dreaming his modest church and grave would one day be almost a shrine of the nations, a holy place in poetry.

What has Shakespeare to show? Only his poetry. That

poetry, by universal esteem, ranks high among the best man
has created.

How then can we account for this man's greatness? Not so
great in his own day as were Ben Jonson and Spenser and
others, time, the greatest and last critic of them all, has
steadily exalted his lines, especially from the early nineteenth
century on, until they are equalled now only by Milton's, and
sparingly by them. What is the answer to the riddle?

Strange that all the critics have steadily ignored the contemporary hints that could resolve the mystery. Two minds,
and two of the greatest, one contemporary and the other almost contemporary to Shakespeare's, have given clear indi-
cations of the source of Shakespeare's greatness; and these
the critics, with all the learned lumber in their heads, have
constantly missed. Ben Jonson, keenest seventeenth-century
writer and collaborator with Shakespeare, actor in his plays,
who lived beyond him and became his sponsor, wrote of the
man from the Avon in the verses which usher the first complete Shakespeare into the world, in 1623. He speaks out au-
thoritatively and clearly: "Sweet swan of Avon." Not a city
mind, but a country one. Not an European internationalist like
Ben Jonson himself, but a man with the green of the country
meadows and streams on his being. Not a bird of wisdom,
like the owl of Athena, or the eagle of Jove; but a pastoral
bird, a bird most at home on sylvan waters, the son of still
waters. Though admitting Shakespeare's "small Latin and
less Greek," Ben Jonson ranks his late friend ahead of witty
Lyly, "sporting Kyd," and Marlowe of the "mighty line."
He makes the allowances that must be made for genius.
And then the poet-critic goes on and puts his finger on the

very key critics have groped for these hundred and fifty years:

> Nature herself was proud of his designs
> And joyed to wear the dressing of his lines.

William Shakespeare was, as we would put it now in one of the sharpest and best of our colloquialisms, a "natural." He has the sweetness of the rustic in him. He has something better than all learning and golden books and high and secret codes of philosophy and disciplines of letters. He has the great green book of nature. He moves on the green carpet. He has the grace of the wind and the sun on him. It took the city man Jonson to see this central fact in Shakespeare, his earthiness, his yeomanliness.

Notice how often Shakespeare's other contemporaries, as well as Jonson, speak of him as "gentle." It is a courtesy and kindness not bred into the man, but born in him. It is the disarming spirit of naturalness, forever the superior to all etiquettes and disciplines. These contemporaries, with Jonson, too, speak often of Shakespeare's writing easily—too easily often for them—by the light of nature.

But John Milton, a little later than Jonson, is more specific still: Shakespeare's art is not a "slow-endeavoring art;" his numbers flow naturally. And then Milton puts *his* finger on the central secret of Shakespeare's greatness, as squarely as Jonson did; and it is an exact corroboration of Jonson's verdict:

> Or sweetest Shakespeare, Fancy's child,
> Warble his native wood-notes wild.

The rustic Shakespeare. Shakespeare's power is a green good one; it comes from the woods, from the country, where he was nurtured; it is a native, a natural one. His song is easy as the bird's. It is one more of the pleasures of the countryside.

There has never been a hint more thoroughly and consistently *not* taken than this that shines so clear in the couplet from *L'Allegro*. Here is the answer to our questions and the resolution of our paradox.

Unlike the great Neo-Greeks, Corneille and Racine, unlike the old Greeks, Sophocles and Aeschylus, Shakespeare has no schedule of the absolutes or philosophical abstracts of life, the over-arching prime movers of men, such as Milton himself loved and sang about. He has little to say directly on the abstract of justice, on temperance, courage, endurance, moderation, religion itself or philosophy; there is no mysticism, no theology, no myths of culture in him, no morality, as there is no polity, no statecraft. Instead, there are only the particular manifestations of these great principles of life in practical living such as can be found in the economy and callings of country folk. It is rule-of-thumb philosophy. Shakespeare's morality is that of the well-managed farm, or the well-articulated trade. His religion is that of the practitioners of life, and it smells of green fields. His polity is the polity that can be learned from the bee-hive and the sheepfold. His community is the community of the green carpet.

So, having only a rural culture behind him, Shakespeare transfers it to the courts of princes; he transfers that green good thing to history, puts his kings and queens down on the green carpet and makes them play their parts of good husbandmen or bad, good mechanics or poor, good shepherds or bad ones. Shakespeare's strength comes from the woods, the rural economies of his Warwickshire; it comes from the crops and crafts, from animal husbandry, from the proverbs of thrift and good management, from the weather, from the virtues of seeds and seasons. His kings do not know it, but they are being saved; they are being tied in with the state-craft of nature; they are being made a part of Spring and Autumn, of works and days, of stars and winds, the sun and the rain. They are being translated to greener kingdoms that do not fade out in the fierce light of time. They are being turned into yeomen.

Through this Elizabethan dramatist over a thousand years of green human experience in agricultural England are speaking. Behind Shakespeare's words are the accumulated voices of thousands of men who have learned to get along with their weather, with the seasons of the year, with night and day, seedtime and harvest, labor with grain and plants, with the rewards and retributions of hard work and sloth, of foresight and carelessness. These are the voices of men who have learned the culture of trees and animals, the equity of the plowed field; the voices of men who have learned by heart the thousand and one poems and disciplines a country-man learns from all the days of his years.

Instead of the fine-spun Platonism of Spenser and Spenser's mediaeval courtly etiquettes and patterns of the life aristocratic and on horseback, Shakespeare gives us some-thing finer: the gospels of goodness and evil of the man for-ever on foot, walking into wisdom behind his oxen, coming into wisdom with his hair bleached out by age and sun and his hands gnarled with the sheaves. It is a more enduring and lovelier etiquette than the doomed man in armor could bequeath us; it is a more enduring and beautiful thing than the pure idea of Plato. For it is poetry, and it is for all ages.

Shakespeare traffics in eternals more surely than Plato. He gives us the history under history, the substance under the pomps and pageantry of war and the law. His patterns are the patterns of fields greening towards Spring, growing golden in Summer, turning russet in Autumn, and graying and whitening towards Winter. He offers men fitting themselves into the calendar, learning by rule-of-thumb, learning from living itself. His kings and dukes, at heart, can be no more than good husbandmen or bad; for the life of the husbandman is what lies deepest at the heart of this poet of Warwickshire; it is his learning, his substitute for Milton's cosmography and Spenser's ritualisms of chivalry, Jonson's sense of the center; Shakespeare's book is the green carpet. In place of the lace and sables and furs of the world of James the First and Charles the First, in place of the wit of men taught by the urban Juvenal and Horace, in place of the courtly Neo-Platonic cult of Henrietta Maria, in place of the intricacies of Court decorums and delights, this man gives us the providence of pastures, the equity of the green fields, the disciplines of the well-kept sheep, the jurisprudence of plows and sheep-crooks, the etiquettes of housewives and housemaids.

Behind William Shakespeare are a hundred generations of British yeomen. He is the yeomanly poet; he sings the country as the state and estate of man as Virgil sings the city. The yeomanly Shakespeare.

Small wonder this poet has lasted and grown taller while

Ben Jonson with all his intimate knowledges of seventeenth-century London and European culture upon him has retreated into the dust of libraries. Ben Jonson's very learning and his full and expert knowledge of the local colors of his London, his very strengths, have crippled him. His page must be shortened with footnotes, for his London has gone out of date. No wonder that Shakespeare grows greener and fresher as the years go by. He does not depend on books or the ephemeral colors of cities. His colors are the rainbows, the umber of ripening grain and the siennas, not of Van Dyck, but of the plowland. These are lasting colors. They weather well. Time cannot fade them. The rich colors of the brightest courts fade out. Polity and politics change and turn into archaeology. Kings go out of fashion. There are few such beings today under the sun. Cities crumble. But Shakespeare's colors are the colors of the Spring and its daffodils and violets, of the greenwood tree and the greenwood, the azure of sky, and the tan on yeomen's faces. Yeomen and shepherds, sheep and roses are still on the face of the earth. William Shakespeare, like Robert Herrick, has been saved by his green wisdoms, his subjects, the perennials of blossoms and harvests. As long as pastures and plowlands last, Shakespeare will last.

The rural economy in Shakespeare is that of the heart of England, Warwickshire, rich in prosperous and sturdy yeomanry, in independence and temperance learned from fruitful labor in fertile soil, rich in fleeces, rich in good craftsmen and artisans to this present day. You can go there and see Shakespeare's kings and queens. A central fact, a metonymy of all the long green history of green England, merry England, is this Warwickshire. Its high painted fields have outlasted the brocades of Elizabeth the Queen; its rank, dark woodlands have outlasted the velvets of Sidney and Essex. Small wonder Shakespeare presents the solid earthy virtues and high animal spirits of Englishmen; strength, stolidity, and calmness; and their natural counterparts, courage, endurance, and generosity of mind, are built into him. He *is* Warwickshire. And Warwickshire is center of the green carpet which is rural England, of a green carpet which is wide as this world.

Yet how could a man who lived so brief a boyhood and youth on this green carpet which is essentially England carry with him such a richness of country lore and wisdom into the city and put it into the poetry for a city stage?

The secret is the secret of folk-sense and folk-memory. Shakespeare's experience of the green meadows along the Avon and in the sheepfolds of Shottery *is* brief. But the experience that keeps his lines forever green is long; it is not his personal experience; it is that of a long line of yeomen ancestors who bred him his bones and marrow. It is not Shakespeare's experience, as Housman says of his folk-sadness; it is man's. Through him the silent tongues of generations of countrymen find a tongue; through him the voices of unnumbered workers of the soil, breeders of cattle and sheep, artists at fitting themselves and their wills and ways into the weather and seasons. Shakespeare's rustic richness is the cumulative experience of many men. That there is such a thing as a folk-memory Shakespeare proves. No one man

[109]

could ever hope to amass the felicities of metaphor and pithy gnomic phrase that Shakespeare shows; it took generations of men to gather the materials and magic of his lines.

To prove this, one has only to cite the proverbs and the proverb-like way of writing when Shakespeare is writing at his best. His mind moves in ageless summaries of experience, timeless and tried wisdoms in the hard tangibles and particulars of life. Take from his poetry the adages, the wise concretes of folk-lore and wisdom, and more than half of Shakespeare's richness and eloquence will go. Take from him the rule-of-thumb application of precepts, his sense of the tangibility of the good life, which is grounded in folk-experience as his folk-proverbs are, and other vast eloquences will disappear. On his wrist as he writes in his London chamber, dark and alone, the hands of many dead and bright men, with the light of running water and sunny sky on them, are guiding his hand as it goes along the page. He is not alone. All Warwickshire yeomen are with him, pouring their vigor into him and his words. Centuries of living out in the winds and weather, out in the cycle of the seasons, in snows and blows, in sowing and reaping, are sparkling in his lines and keeping them alive. Beside such live brightness Spenser's bookish brightness seems dead and lustreless. Shakespeare's experience is a divine average of common men's experience of getting along well in a green northern place, where sunshine is brief but potent, mornings are an exclamation of wonder, where long twilights bring sadness, and long nights and Winters are like men's discontents. Shakespeare lays down no law but he buttresses it about with an instant countryman's application,

> The quality of mercy is not strain'd,
> It droppeth as the gentle rain from heaven . . .

His Elizabethan exuberance often makes the country coloration of the idea double,

> I am a tainted wether of the flock,
> Meetest for death: the weakest kind of fruit
> Drops earliest to the ground, and so let me.

It is not a city man, not Antonio, speaking; it is a long pageant of Warwickshire farmers and shepherds using Antonio's lips for their hard-won wisdom. Shakespeare's language is full of the country, even when it comes from princes' mouths. Kings talk like his "sunburnt sicklemen;" queens like queens "of curds and cream." His best language moves in the terms of the household and husbandry, in herbs and simples. The fairy lore alone shows where a vast deal of Shakespeare's poetry comes from: from the tavern and the kitchen. This poetry is of the earth, earthy.

No one man wrote Shakespeare surely. Not Sir Francis Bacon. Not Edward de Vere. Not Shakespeare. It is the many-instanced tongue of many downright men speaking at once out of long practice of patience, hard work, and accurate observation. It is, at its best—and Shakespeare's language is oftener at its best than that of almost any other poet in our tongue—folk-language or a language rooted in the folk-experience. It is the lasting language of concretes. It is full of sharp, hard objects as the old Anglo-Saxon is. Intangibles, precepts, codes have little place in it; all precepts are shored up by practices. The tangibles of Winter and Summer, twilight and dawn are in it, night's candles, the canker in the rose, the whetting of the sickle, the bleat of sheep. It is a *thing*-poetry, not an *idea*-poetry. It is not surprising that Voltaire and other Frenchmen, whose minds are always filled with nice foliations of exquisite imponderables of logic and philosophy, think of Shakespeare as a barbarian. He is so full of kitchen stuff, garden stuff, homeliness and concreteness, so full of *objects,* that he offends their sense of good taste and decorum. He mixes majesty with matter too often. The French want the poetry in the mouths of great people greatly feeling to be greatly filled with excellent absolutes; this talking of noblemen and noble women which is so like that of farmers and artisans and shepherdesses astounds and irks them. Make no mistake. The over-arching of the absolute is there in Shakespeare; but the Frenchman finds the language that affirms it impure and tasting of earth. In our ears, though, it is the greatest language in poetry. It reminds us of the *Bible;* for that, too, is a book of long English poetry, of many average yeomenly minds speaking through the English translators of it from Alfred the Great's translator through Wiclif, Coverdale, and Tyndale. It is the poetry of concretes of this good green earth: lambs and lamps, loaves and sheaves, sickle and hammer, the cup, the table, the vine, the rock, the path, green pastures, and still waters.

Shakespeare's is the tongue Englishmen speak most when most excited, most calm, and most passionate. It is the language Wordsworth wanted to find, but did not always succeed in finding, in his lyrics. But, believe it, it is there. It is still there in the English countryside as it was in Shakespeare's day and long before.

This language is a language rooted in the seasons, colored by weather, metaphored with night and day, growth and decay, elemented with the elements, burned by the sun and stained by the soil. It is a noble tongue, not of Greek or of mediaeval aristocrats, but of noble husbandmen and herdsmen, noble mechanics and hunters and groomsmen and shepherds, on their best behavior, in their best clothes, the clothes of proverbs and wise sayings. It is the speech of artists who have learned to handle tools well, their creatures, their horses and hounds, their houses. It is popular in the very best sense. It is the language Englishmen are begot in, christened in, that they take their sport in, build their homes in, woo in, marry in, the language they are buried in. If the folk be left out of Shakespeare's lines, and only the law allowed to remain, and bare nobles and kings, scant little, precious little will be left.

Here are no etiquettes of mediaeval chivalric society, though many of these characters are mediaeval rulers of men; here are no books of the courtier, but earth's downrights from green fields and barn and byre. The talk is of tools, of spades and wellsprings of water. King Henry VI, who likely did not know a water-pump from a hand-saw, speaks easily of newfangled pumps that have some buckets going down empty as full ones are coming up. King Richard II does as well, as he plays with his crown:

> Here, cousin . . .
> On this side my hand, and on that side yours.

Now is this golden crown like a deep well
That owes two buckets, filling one another;
The emptier ever dancing in the air,
The other down, unseen, and full of water:
That bucket down and full of tears am I,
Drinking my griefs, whilst you mount up on high.

Here is the clank of chains, the whine of wheels, country
calls and rural ejaculations. A king deposed can wish no
handsomer wish to the king who has deposed him than to
wish him a good store of "many years of sunshine days."
Here is a language of bedrock meteorology and bedrock
morality. An England torn apart by the Wars of the Roses
is a flower-garden overrun by caterpillars and weeds:

> Our sea-walled garden, the whole land
> Is full of weeds, her fairest flowers chok'd up,
> Her fruit-trees all unprun'd, her hedges ruin'd,
> Her knots disorder'd, and her wholesome herbs
> Swarming with caterpillars.

And the Duke of York's gardener can wish no better wish
than a good gardener's wish that his king had been a good
gardener, too:

> Oh! what pity is it
> That he hath not so trimm'd and dress'd his land
> As we this garden! We at time of year
> Do wound the bark, the skin of our fruit-trees,
> Lest, being over-proud in sap and blood,
> With too much riches it confound itself:
> Had he done so to great and growing men,
> They might have liv'd to bear, and he to taste
> Their fruits of duty. Superfluous branches

We lop away, that bearing boughs may live:
Had he done so, himself had borne the crown,
Which waste of idle hours hath quite thrown down.

This sorry King Richard himself of this sorry England cannot be untangled from meteorology; from Spring and Fall:

He that hath suffer'd this disorder'd Spring
Hath now himself met with the Fall of leaf.

Kings and Winters are coalesced; queens are not to be sep-
arated from roses and apple blooms. An unhappy monarch
is like a cloudy sunrise; England's dust is laid by showers of
blood; rulers rain foul weather from their weeping eyes. A
dying duke's mouth is full of rural proverbs as he describes
a profligate king:

Violent fires soon burn out themselves;
Small showers last long, but sudden storms are short;
He tires betimes that spurs too fast betimes.

Dukes talk like yeomen; and yeomen talk like kings. The
practical, the countrified wisdom pours from every mouth,
noble or common:

Things sweet to taste prove in digestion sour.

An evil soul is like "a goodly apple rotten at the heart."
"Pitchers have ears"—this from the lips of a queen. A duke,
dying, recalls his animal husbandry:

Deal mildly with his youth;
For young hot colts, being rag'd, do rage the more.

[115]

The air of the Court, the fields of battle are filled with proverbs: "Idle weeds are fast in growth;" "Short Summers lightly have a forward Spring;" a "good pasture makes fat sheep."

The green earth is never out of the mind of this poet of the yeomen. The process of the seasons is never forgotten for long. Leave the meteorology out of Shakespeare's sonnets of love, and little will be left to distinguish that love.

> When I do count the clock that tells the time,
> And see the brave day sunk in hideous night;
> When I behold the violet past prime,
> And sable curls all silver'd o'er with white;
> When lofty trees I see barren of leaves,
> Which erst from heat did canopy the herd,
> And Summer's green all girded up in sheaves,
> Borne on the bier with white and bristly beard;
> Then of thy beauty do I question make,
> That thou among the wastes of time must go,
> Since sweets and beauties do themselves forsake
> And die as fast as they see others grow;
>   And nothing 'gainst Time's scythe can make defence
>   Save breed, to brave him when he takes thee hence.

Passions wax and wane with the moon, march with the seasons, come to fruition with the fruit. It is the sequent eloquence of the calendar; it is the logic of flowers; the religion of green and golden earth, brown and white earth, earth wheeling through its year and dancing the brave chorals of night and day.

I say we have met this language of Shakespeare before. It

is in our English *Bible*. It is a good language, good in tangibles, rich in concretes. The matters of man's salvation are to be found most in proverbs and parables, most of them from the good green carpet. It is not like the tongue of Plato, rich in words of starry significances and measurements of the law; it is, like the Hebrews' tongue, the language of the people, of the carpenters, the makers of bread and raisers of wool, of fishermen, of the tillers of the soil. Its richness is the richness of metaphor and metonymy; and its metaphors are the threshing-floor, the leaf, the loaf, salt, the gourd, the net, lambs, the foxes, the flowers of the world. It is the old tongue of our Anglo-Saxon ancestors. It is the tongue of a people who have lived a long time on the carpet that is forever green.

Shakespeare's kings and queens in their extremities, when most moved, on the edge of battle, on the edge of doom, *in articulo mortis,* speak like no kings of Court; the enamel of history breaks brittle from them, they emerge and speak like plain Warwickshire shepherds and Warwickshire yeomen, like English housewives. They speak the tongue of experts in weather and tools. Justice is white-headed wheat. Equity is the straight furrow. Polity is the good of the sheep.

A king in his purple sits him down on a molehill in the midst of a civil war. He opens his mouth, and the first words to come out of it are meteorology and simile:

> This battle fares like to the morning's war,
> When dying clouds contend with growing light,
> What time the shepherd, blowing of his nails,
> Can neither call it perfect day nor night.

[117]

On the Green Carpet

In his discouragement and woe, this old king turns into a Warwickshire shepherd. Shakespeare, in the midst of history, suddenly comes to everlasting life, and bursts into the finest pastoral poem so far. Nothing in Virgil or Theocritus is so good. It is many centuries of cumulative peace among flocks, such as produced the *Psalms* and *Proverbs,* speaking through Shakespeare's mouth. Listen:

> Here on this molehill will I sit me down.
> To whom God will, there be the victory!
> For Margaret my queen, and Clifford, too,
> Have chid me from the battle; swearing both
> They prosper best of all when I am thence.
> Would I were dead! if God's good will were so;
> For what is in this world but grief and woe?

(When Shakespeare rhymes two lines, you can expect something final or especially magnificent, and he will not disappoint us this time. Here it comes)

> O God! methinks it were a happy life
> To be no better than a homely swain;
> To sit upon a hill, as I do now,
> To carve out dials quaintly, point by point,
> Thereby to see the minutes how they run,—
> How many make the hour full complete;
> How many hours bring about the day;
> How many days will finish up the year;
> How many years a mortal man may live.
> When this is known, then to divide the times,—
> So many hours must I tend my flock;
> So many hours must I take my rest;
> So many hours must I contemplate;

So many hours must I sport myself;
So many days my ewes have been with young;
So many weeks ere the poor fools will ean;
So many years ere I shall shear the fleece:
So minutes, hours, days, months, and years,
Pass'd over to the end they were created,
Would bring white hairs unto a quiet grave.

There is poetry the like of which, for calm, for flow, for beauty of concreteness, is not elsewhere to be matched this side of the *Twenty-Third Psalm*. This isn't an Elizabethan, a Spenser or a Jonson, speaking. This is a world poet speaking to the world, long ago, now, for the far future.

Of course, Shakespeare is an Elizabethan in wanting to do a good thing twice over. So now, in this chronicle play, he goes on and does it. He puts another pastoral poem into this late Henry's mouth, just before—with Elizabethan prolixity again—he has a young soldier drag in a man he has slain and discover it to be his father, and, following this, to out-Herod Herod, presents an old father dragging in a slain man who, when he is unhelmeted, proves to be his only son! This second pastoral is not nearly so good as the first, but it is still a good green thing; and, hurriedly, just before the groundlings in the Globe begin to reach for missiles to throw maybe, Shakespeare becomes a modern and writes a few phrases Robert Frost might envy:

Ah, what a life were this! how sweet; how lovely!
Gives not the hawthorn bush a sweeter shade
To shepherds, looking on their silly sheep,
Than doth a rich embroider'd canopy

To kings that fear their subjects' treachery?
O, yes, it doth; a thousand-fold it doth.
And to conclude,—the shepherd's homely curds,
His cold thin drink out of his leathern bottle,
His wonted sleep under a fresh tree's shade,
All which secure and sweetly he enjoys,
Is far beyond a prince's delicates,
His viands sparkling in a golden cup,
His body couched in a curious bed,
When care, mistrust, and treason wait on him.

Less rich and learned than Spenser, less disciplined and even less artistic than Jonson, inferior Elizabethan that he is to them, Shakespeare none the less has written poetry with greater eloquence and lasting power in this changing, becoming world of ours. He grows stronger with the centuries. He grows stronger because he never got too high into the rarefied atmosphere of morality, polity, or philosophy to be long away from his touch, like Antaeus', with the re-creating green earth. He is the Antaeus of poets; he is constantly renewed by his matter. As long as there are farms, as long as there are shepherds and sheepfolds, as long as there are trees and flowers, he will grow stronger. He wrote history, a poetry full of princes, but not a poetry of princes. It is a poetry of man, common earthy man, with his head, in the hour of his agony, full of apples and fleece, running water and blowing roses, and peace that comes from a man's making peace with night and day and the seasons, with sweat and work, in the outdoors, where a happy farm is a small kingdom that outlasts all the kingdoms of kings who ever wore crowns. His men are crowned with sage lealty and fealty to the calen-

dar and the callings of working men living on the green carpet and going to their long rest beneath it, when their time
is on them, serenely. Men out under the sun and moon. Men
handsome as tanned haycocks, fields white with wheat, the
roses of the winds on their cheeks, snow on their heads that
all men must expect on them in the snow's season.

Shakespeare's men are men of our North, where the Summers are brief but very fragrant and very full of birds and
wild roses; where the Fall comes like a man's waning in
vigor, with sadness; where wind hard as time, in its time,
strips men of their strength, and a bitter sound of death is in
the ears. The lovely chorals of our distinctive seasons are his
poetry; good men experienced in the outdoors, good women
experienced in herbs and healing flowers, in beauty for use.
As long as good outdoors men and the seasons, and the green
carpet itself that produces these, shall last, the poetry of
Shakespeare will endure.

"Sweetest Shakespeare." Milton was, as so often, right.
Sweetness is the word. It is the sweetness of honey, of loam
turned fresh over in the strong sunlight, of blowing apple
trees, the sweetness of strong men plowing and lambs leaping
with Spring. Shakespeare's best book was not any in print;
it was the green folio of the country where the seasons write
the changing lines and wise laws are laid down for the good
life of man. One of Shakespeare's best dukes, who had turned
from the Court and the life artificial, says as much:

> This our life, exempt from public haunt,
> Finds tongues in trees, books in the running brooks,
> Sermons in stones, and good in everything.

On the Green Carpet

Small wonder Shakespeare was a common traveller in the Conestoga wagons going west in America; he was at home among men of the soil and the seasons. Such men recognized their own poetry when they heard it. They knew their poetry, writing those centuries of years, over there in England, over here in the early agricultural America. They were men like kings as their remote Anglo-Saxon forebears had been, even when dunging their fields and shearing their fleeces. Shakespeare's cloak of the courtly story did not hide his sweet commonness and his essential rustic rightness from them. "Perilous in common folk," Sir John Froissart once called the English people. They are. The yeomen proved it on the French knights at Crécy and Agincourt. Shakespeare, uncommon commoner poet, proves it. One may expect a Prince Hal from the barley-patch; a Prince Hamlet from the cottage; kings from the sheepcot. And such monarchs of the people, created by the people of the green carpet, for the people on all green carpets the world around, keep their democratic glory and do not fade out under the suns of the years.

∾ IV ∾
THE NEW ENGLAND GREEN

4. *The New England Green*

A man speaks best of what he knows best. There is one corner of the wide green carpet that I want to turn to now. For, having spoken at large so far, of the vast reaches of poetry, I desire to go home now, to go into particulars, to go small, to go home. From now on I shall narrow the area I cover of this carpet of the good and enduring green. Each chapter shall narrow in and, I hope, go deeper into this theme of nature—the good green nature—in poetry.

I am a New Englander, and I am going home. This small, rocky and hilly, and rather infertile and cold part of the northern green carpet has been my home for a long time; and so, from custom, I may say what I have to say with more authority and maybe with more eloquence. New England has been home to me for over three hundred years. For I am child enough still, and poet, to believe that life is not so simply measured by one lifetime and that it does not begin with one's first steps, but was there mightily and magnificently before one took those first steps, was in those first steps, and will not break off with one's last. The older I grow, the more certain I grow that a man lives backward and forward of his here and now, more than he ever lives in the now, and has a familiar hand holding his own as he goes. I believe that what a man is he has been for a long, long time, that what he

is will continue a long time after his time. I could not be a
poet and not believe that.

I can prove this with A. E. Housman; I have already
proved it with William Shakespeare. The best green parts of
Shakespeare's lines were written for him by his yeomanly
forebears, men of Warwickshire, at England's green heart,
men of sheep and barns and tools, who worked up his metaphors and myths for him, worked up his analogies and his
proverbs for him, by running the straight lines of their furrows and working their acres well and being good shepherds
of their sheep.

So for the eight generations and the ten generations of
fathers and mothers before I happened as a repeated son, I
have been growing accustomed to the New England I am
learning little by little to live in and believe in now. I have
been finding my repeated way about life and Cape Cod
farmhouses and seafolks' taller ones; learning what doors
lead to what, what windows look out upon what necessary
sights there are to see. A poet's forerunners in his place, the
air and the soil and the sky of his place, write the poet's
deepest parts to his poems for him. In this larger house
studded by the seasons and ceilinged over with the stars and
moon, the New England country, I have been familiarizing
myself with more bountiful and enduring pantries, green
cupboards and kitchens and parlors than any New England
house has, that go less out of date as the winds come and go,
the snow blows, and the sun shines after the rain. Outdoors
and in, I hope I am a wiser and more generous housekeeper
for my three centuries of growing to feel at home, with my

ɔuses, my hills, my woods and fields, my people, and my
a.

So let me return home and say the things I have learned
home.

Every little while, people—well-meaning people, too—
ather for our New England funeral. The windows are dark-
ned, the wisest and strongest are gone, the sound of the
rasshoppers is over the land, the sound of the milking low,
ɪe well is dry and the bucket broken, the flour barrel is low,
nd the mourners go about the streets. It is sad, but this is
ɪe way the world goes. This is the end. New England was
 splendid thing—if a little cold and aloof—while it lasted.
'his now is goodbye to New England. A chapter, and an
nportant one—if a little too often brushed by stardust and
ncomfortable divinity—is closed in American literature. No
ɔuntry can expect to have two Hawthornes, or a second
merson. And a Bronson Alcott would be just too much!

So the neighbors come in to bury us decently. The accounts
re closed. One knows where Longfellow and Melville, Low-
ll and Whittier, are now, nights. And days. And years. And
fter-years—oh, especially after-years. It is for good. For bet-
ɛr or worse. But they are all gone. Now the critics of litera-
ɪre, all the accounts being nicely balanced up, debits and
redits settled and arranged, can turn from the Atlantic
chool of American literature, so neatly summed up and
igeonholed, and give their full attention to the Middle
tates, the Middle West, the Deep South, the far Golden
ɔast, and follow the further developments of our literature
n its logical journey, along with the center of population or

the economic apex, the hum of industry, of wheels and cattl
and coin, or the ferment of politics, west. Westward, like th
course of empire, American literature takes its way.

It is nice—and I use the word exactly—to have eras of li
erature end in time. Chaucer and Dryden show good sens
in choosing to die at a century's turn. Shakespeare doesn't, th
more's the pity. But he almost does with his writing life; h
runs over only a decade into a seventeenth century where h
does not belong. Even queens, Elizabeth and Victoria, wh
name literary periods, are almost as nice about such things.

Yet, for all that, literature has a way of doubling bach
lingering on, beginning over, coming up again in plac
safely dead. Coming out of graves. Out of fields alread
harvested. And this is particularly and peculiarly the provinc
and habit of New England. It has always been so, come t
think of it. From the sure dialectic of Mather and Edward
safely sepulchered, strange new vines spring, which Jonatha
Edwards and Cotton Mather would have shuddered at, win
their tendrils around insignificant man, and lift him to th
stars. A Calvinistic Jehovah, cabined in a geometry of divin
ity as snug as anything in Euclid, grows out into a Tran
scendental governor of an expanded universe in which curve
of personality are often the shortest lines to glory, and con
mon man the uncommonest and most complex creature c
them all.

The critics had no sooner put Emerson and Longfellow t
rest, and turned their minds to younger and rougher Amer
cans, Mark Twain and Whitman, than up came a whole new
crop of writers in a place where the hay was all cut and ha
vested safely in. And this aftermath, this second mowing, in

ludes at least three figures of poets who will have to be reckned with in not only future American literature but in the terature of the world. Robinson, Millay, Frost, all three nurred on run-out acres, are all rich with a new kind of richss, not known to the Victorian New England, but known nd esteemed in the larger world, a richness out of time as vell as definitely local to New England and of our time. It is oo bad. The critics will have to reopen the account. New ngland is still in literary history.

Apparently there must be something fairly permanent and airly and permanently vigorous in this unprepossessing, ocky corner of a rich continent to account for this continuus crop of creative impulses these last one hundred years and nore. Suppose, now, I try, with my three-hundred-year-old yes long practiced in observing New England kindly and ritically, to tell what I believe this yeast is that keeps workng New England into new literary loaves (I hope you will orgive a figure from the kitchen where Lowell would never o for a serious figure, maybe) every so often. There must be omething still in the run-down, farmed-out but handsome ld place to breed and feed new poets. Surely there is some ierce fecundity here, some seed which the wilderness, that has retty well taken back upper New England, and which the actories and Summer vacationists (the Victorians called hem rusticators) that have pretty well taken over the southrn parts of these smallest of the United States, cannot choke ut. Let us see if we can discover what these vigors or seeds re.

New England, of course, always has bulked larger than its esources warrant. That is the first essence of New England-

ness anyway. Life has always had to go up. There was r
other place to go. As most of New England seems uphill
the outsider, it may be here, right at the start of our explor
tion, we have an essential metaphor. Sons have always b
lieved that they must rise above their fathers; mothers ha
always been proud of daughters who have improved on the
in culture and charity. Improvement, advance—there is r
way forward but up. This goes for intellects as well as sho
and watches. It is a land of better and better morals as we
as better mousetraps. It all makes me think of an aunt I h
who never rested from culture; she tired me and the comm
nity dreadfully. First it was her manners, then her voice, the
her mind. Finally, it was her morals. She would not ha
been a New Englander if she hadn't brought up again
those. Her morals she never did catch up to; to the other
she did. And with her it was other people's morals as well
her own. That's another New England essentiality.

If paradoxes are the beginnings of the life creative, then
first glance at New England will show we are pretty like
to be creative. Paradoxes flourish, with us, two-three to tl
acre, thicker and better even than our apple trees or our bee
They are everywhere you look. Small farmers living in bi
houses; large churches for tiny or non-existent villages; fi
houses at a crossroads, called Paris; big ideas coming out
little hamlets called Athens, Mexico, Norway, Bethel, Lo
don, or Peru. Maybe it is the big names: we feel we have
grow up to our village's title—Unity, Friendship, Harmon
Shiloh, Bethel, Dublin; Concord or Providence; Lebanon an
New Boston. Anyway, people try to live up to the vast.
town burns up in one of our recent and frequent forest-fire

nd the people meet and decide to build a church before they
ut up a single house, or bank, or schoolhouse. In the older
lays, the people build the schoolhouse on their poorest half-
cre, all ledges, where the crows have to bring their lunches
rom the ocean and break them open on the hard rock; and
et the people expect the children to grow rich and fertile
n their minds; and they do! For these are New England
oys and girls, used to getting sustenance out of places mostly
ure stone, and they are disciplined to the idea of going up
n life.

The hard-pressed New England farmers expect the worst
f their weather; and their expectations are amply rewarded.
t comes a killing frost in June or August; it rains pitchforks
n the mown hay; it rains all Spring so they cannot get a
eed in by Decoration Day, the deadline for our gardens, and
hen their corn and beans catch it from an early black-frost
n September. When it should snow, it comes off a thaw and
ains; and our apple trees wake up to their peril in mid-
Winter, and we can't get our oxen—we still use the beasts
Abraham and Laban leaned on, since it is a case of have-to—
nto the woods to haul out pine logs, and they rot through a
ear. We look for an April shower, and we get a February
lizzard. And yet, glory be, and there being a glory not only
f rainbows but rewards of untimely weather in New England, the cussedness of the weather often is the making of
what few beans or peas we raise. And backward meteorology
proves, it may be, the presence of some sort of governor somewhere out among the stars. Snow can be the poor farmer's
only effective dressing. It can account for his one margin of
safety:

Poor Man's Dressing

On budded April falls the blessing,
White and deep, the poor-man's dressing
Falls from the sky on hungry farms
That lean hard on everlasting arms.

Snow falls on steep farms mostly stones
And makes a thin broth out of bones,
This New England backward weather
Keeps farmers' skins and bones together.

Farmers need not fertilize
Very much, their low-hung skies
Do it for them, which fact will
Prove God runs New England still.

Late snow does something deep, its spells
Maybe free trace-minerals,
Cobalt and such, make stones relent
To apples of honey and heaven blent.

These farmers never have manna or quail
Fall on them, but snow and hail,
If they come late and cranky enough,
Are just as providential stuff.

So out of tribulation snow
The extra beans in the steep row,
Good health in the corn that lights
Houses with popcorn Winter nights.

Maybe it's cobalt, after all,
Look behind the pasture wall

The New England Green

Where the late snow lay knee-high—
Bluets are there like fallen sky.

It is all very puzzling to the outsider, and providential. We have to farm on rock; and we get rock-like sons who make good founders of cities and industries out west, if not here. A good railroad builder grows up in a place where the moose till tread out some of the roads with their wide hooves. My mother could not take daylight time ever to make her flower-garden. But she took the hours of night, worked over bulbs and rose-slips by the light of her kitchen lamp set down on the floor of the starry world; and her roses still live, where all her daylight children, her strawberry plants and goose-berries have gone into green oblivion in the forest; her white, single narcissus-flowers, set out by night in her leisure time, still blossom in their three white circles each May, blossom in spite of being swallowed up in the forest, and face the witch-grass and firs that try to crowd them into death, fight them back, and still live. Strange. We learn to read books as children from the trade-names on mowing-machines; I my-self learned my letters, between blueberry pies, from the hot letters on our Wood-Bishop-Bangor-Maine cookstove's oven-door.

These paradoxes of our northern place make good poems; they have the makings of poems in them, in any case. They are an earnest of that fertility I am looking for.

Our New England, for all its size, still bulks large in our national life, as it did all through our past history. It still raises fine educations. Its colleges, universities, and schools, private and public, are still standard. Not professional educa-

[135]

tion so much—though there is the best technical school or
the banks of the Charles maybe in the world—as liberal. Edu-
cation that sets free. Wherever liberal ideas flourish, the soil
is pretty apt to be apt for poetry.

In the older days, New England was the theological center
of our American cosmos, of course. In industry, though mass
manufactures, which it had the Yankee ingenuity to inaugu-
rate, have moved south or west, New England still finds economic salvation in developing ingeniously expert small and
diversified manufactures, as those four-score kinds or more
in Worcester, Massachusetts. Snowshoes, skis, hunting-gear,
lobster traps, boats—it can still make these better than most
places.

But I must omit these New England crops, the theological,
the intellectual, and the industrial. For I am after the more
permanent harvests, the harvests of the creative spirit in poetry.

The materials for poetry are found in abundance in New
England still. Significantly, they seem to increase the farther
you go north of Boston. All three of our major modern
American poets are north-of-Boston ones. This means that
tougher, hardier matter of poetry is found in the greener
northern half of these small United States than in the southern; that is, in the unindustrialized, unurbanized, in the agricultural—or better say, sylvan half; the small-villaged, upper
New England of Maine, New Hampshire, and Vermont,
that part which Professor Toynbee describes as being above
the optimum level of hardship in weather and soil. This is
to say, the part of New England still lovely and lively with
the color green. The green-carpet half—it is nearer two-thirds

—of New England. The beyond-the-optimum land! Maybe poetry has always insisted on being there because of the sweetness of adversity. The new poetry is where the older New Englanders are making their last stand—it is often very much like the first—for man and mind against those careless forgetters, the forest, the frost. Or better put it, as I trust we shall see, where man has made his truce with loneliness and small gardens, small opportunities and large belief in life. It is a green world where much must be still done by hand, sire of all the arts, but where hand-work leaves more time for the head and heart. New England might be defined as the place where farms leave a man time for his heart and head.

Suppose, now, we take a western American, who often does wonder just how this section of our country, whose greatest industries, ships and shoes and cotton cloth, have ebbed away long ago, does manage to survive and play an important part in our nation's culture and letters—indeed, remains as a kind of criterion of American culture—suppose we take this hypothetical Californian or Missourian, Doubting Thomas of an American, who must be shown, into this northern New England of woods and small farms and small villages, and see what he will notice here, and somewhat in the order of his noticing them, as features that may have the essence of culture, the seeds of poetry, in them. I won't vouch for the exact order of these impressions; but, roughly, I think, they will follow the sequence that follows.

Our Westerner will, in his car, be confirmed at once in his leading old impression that New England is a small place. He will be able to go all over it in a day, as he might three or four counties in Texas. But we must insist that he take time. New England is the country and the state of taking time; in talk, in civics, in culture. So while here, the Westerner must take his.

This visitor will subscribe wholeheartedly at first to Toynbee's opinion of us. It is a hard place in weather and lay of the land, in crookedness of roads and poverty of soil. Waterpower and wood and scenery will seem to be the only things greatly in abundance. But the man will drive on, slowly, and gradually he will begin to notice the more important things behind these first impressions. His mind will begin to look at things from new angles, and not merely because his automobile is forever pointing up or down and never horizontally.

Size is really an illusion, the visitor will begin to discover, that is, horizontal size. If this section of the northern Appalachian chain were ironed out, it might cover a larger area than Missouri or even some of the deserts of California. It is an up-and-down country; there are no horizontals but the sea; and its shore, in Maine, is accordion-pleated both horizontally and perpendicularly. There is a lot more to New England than he first thought. Distances between little centers of life are to be measured, not as the crow—and the wise and enduring crow is almost a token of our spirit and our culture—flies, but as the deer trots. The deer also is a totem of our spirit, free and independent and ungregarious, and well proportioned to the winds and weather. Towns that are in each other's sight may have deep mountain valleys or deep estuaries of the ocean in between them. As a boy I was as safe from certain Aztec cousins of mine, though I could see them, as I was from the Mexicans; the ocean between us being what it was. In these perpendicular estrangements of our villages, weather plays a vast part. There are five distinct weatherstrips to northern New England east to west, more than from the Hudson to the Rockies. The Hudson Valley is one, the Connecticut River system is the second, the Merrimac is the third, the Androscoggin and Saco the third, Kennebec and Penobscot the fourth, and Fundy and the Atlantic make the fifth. The weather in each strip is *sui generis;* it will be snowing in one and shining in the next; Summer and peace here, Winter and gales next-door. Within a few miles we are continents apart in weather. But such adversities and discrepancies, multiplied and repeated in our successive days or even hours within these weather-strips, make for character and poems of great individuality.

Geography and meteorology bulk larger here, the Missourian will find, and are more facts of life than elsewhere. There is no security or serenity, here, of the prairie, and, by the same token, no tedium either. Mountains are not merely facts on maps but constant facts for the eyes, the feet, the muscles, the mind. Lakes and freshwater waves are right in the midst of everyday living. Forests cast long shadows on citizens' minds, and towns take on something from having deer and moose at times for visitors, always for near neighbors. Spring is everybody's business because it is so late and good to welcome; a heavy snowstorm often puts large towns back into the Middle Ages or even interplanetary isolation. High winds are visitors all men must make allowances for. Frost is a near neighbor, and cold weather, half of all the years, shapes the contours of all occupations and the contours of all minds. All crops must be housed half the year, all animals and fowls taken into the family. When the white death comes yearly over the land, life must go under cover of shingles and boards, under cover of faith, hope, and charity. The low sun must be annually aided by fire made by man. The untold strengths that come from hard weathers are something a poet can reckon on, though historians like Toynbee may think of hard weather as brutalizing and benumbing and destroying. "Sweet are the uses of adversity"; it is the poet speaking, not the economist; and he is laying down the law for New England apples as well as for poetry. Our mountains of upper New England, though they scarcely provide gold enough for the family wedding rings, are full of enough goodness to make emperors of us all; and the color of an October maple is more golden than gold.

And always, on our east, is the fact of the sea. No Maine man can escape that fact, in gale, in fog, sudden disaster and iron death, but in utter loveliness, too, and vistas, beyond and above every little white or gray house, into infinity, into fear, the beginning of wisdom, into eternity and the possibility, and probability, of an everlasting arm. He who knows and lives with the sea has a music under his feet and a solitude to make him more of a truster in tenderness. He will never lack danger, and he will never lack courage and a sense of the otherwhere always around small boats of men and men's small lives.

From the steep, hard lay of their land, from the hard and abrupt weather they live in, from the loneliness of forests and sadness of the sea, these New England people, our Westerner will discover, have become a hard and deep people. They are practiced in privation and so schooled in faith. The West-

ner will find that there is more to the New Englander than
hat he has in this world or even hopes to have in a next, if
e believes in one. The man has worked out the art—it is an
t, and the most typical and best-articulated one New Eng-
nd has developed—of making the most of what he has, be
beans or being. New England could be, and has been, de-
ribed as the land of doing without. Doing without may
ell be the essential the world most misses now, when states
nslave their citizens to provide them with all the comforts
nd securities which would ruin even a philosopher. Often it
what a New Englander wants that determines the way he
ehaves. Hunger can be a handsome begetter of poems. It is a
andsome whetstone.

There is more to this New Englander than his strength
r colorful routines of existence. Adversity, not Calvin, has
ained him to expect a constant re-birth even in the latest,
rayest years he has. He is tuned to regeneration. He must
urn over new leaves. He is the man who must be born again.
Iis own countryside teaches him to expect the apocalyptical
nd the sudden supernal. His own maples, blazing for
ed and golden miles up and down the Saco and Androscog-
in and sending back all Summer's sunlight in a blue hand-
ul of days, tell this New Englander that much the same
hing is expected of him. His maple tree is his final analogue.
ust behind his tie-up and his comfortable Herefords, sud-
lenly shines the burning bush:

> New Englanders are like the pasture slopes
> Behind their barns. You put them down as sober,
> And then one day you wake up, and you find them
> Red and golden maples of October.

[141]

It takes adversity and coming close
To trouble and hard times to make them glow,
Then they really flower as swamp maples
Flower on the edge of frost and snow.

You might suppose that they were never going
To be much more than middling fair to good,
When suddenly they are new people wholly,
Burning bushes blazing in the wood.

Maybe they had such hard time getting born,
What with the cold and all, they feel they must
Be born again, and so in age and trial
They blossom out of death and out of dust.

They are good people for your nearest neighbors
When the deep old earth's foundation slips,
It is good to have behind the barn
The flame and beauty of the Apocalypse.

But there is that explicit order of successive impressions
the Westerner will have as he traverses the green carpet of
northern New England mountains and woods and farms. I
propose now to follow those impressions in what may be
their natural sequence.

First, I swear, it will be graveyards. The visitor will see
them everywhere. Almost no view of mountain or lake, village or valley, but the white company of the departed New
Englanders will be there. The man from a land so new that
cemeteries are a rarity will be impressed by the ancient dead
of New England. They will loom in his eyes as holders of all
the finest vantages of view; they are on the handsomest hills
overlooking the village; they hold the headlands overhang-

ing the harbor and the sea. To his mind they spoil the fairest prospects. But the living New Englanders will not agree with him. No view is too fine for the old ones; and headlands are windy places, anyway, and not for the living:

Shore Graveyards

Summer people wonder why the best
Hilltops looking out here on the sea
Are taken up by people gone to rest;
The graveyards spoil the sightliest property,
And that, they hold, is poor economy.

Yet there is something, maybe, in this giving
Those who are gone as good things as you can;
And hilltops in high wind are not for living,
Low houses are the best for the fishing man;
It's Summer folks, not natives, want to tan.

In far old times all sailing men took care
To paint sharp eyes upon their ship's sharp prow.
Might happen, in these old graveyards up there
Good eyes are watching over sailing people now.
Graves look well on headlands, anyhow.

The Westerner will silently compute that the dead outnumber the living in this strange land back in the East, back where his antique ancestors had the wisdom, he claims, to emigrate from. Two men in the "bone-orchard," to give the cemetery its proper colloquial New England name, for every one now in the orchard trees picking the fruit. Two dead to one alive—that seems to be about the correct ratio here. The dead everywhere, and everywhere underfoot. Right in the heart of farms, right on the village green, just as right in the center of traffic often in Boston. It must make the living New Englander pull up and shiver to have these *memento mori's* so in his eyes. But the fact of the matter, the poetry of the matter is that it doesn't. It makes him go more vigorously, more thoughtfully and carefully, at whatever he is doing. It keeps him more alive, being so with the dead. For the dead are *his* dead; they are himself a century hence.

Granite's a Model

Two in the bone-orchard should be
For each one in the orchard tree—
That's the proper ratio;
New England's small towns prove it so.

A man will toe the hard mark right
When he is in his grandmother's sight,
Though his grandmother is a granite
Shaft where all who pass may scan it.

Small boys will mind their P's and Q's
And not wade puddles in good shoes
When he who made and loved them lies
Under the grassy hill all eyes.

Ten men quiet for one in love;
When straight old good men lie above
A white town they kept neat as a pin,
It will be hard for a man to sin.

New England dead are not the dead,
They are judges of heart and head;

And he who knows them has a start
On a character and a heart.

It's no wonder New England raises
Good men common as white daisies;
The best ones here are granite stones,
And granite's a model for young bones.

So what seems to the outsider a defect is really a virtue. Poetry's great business is to keep the hands of the dead and the living and the unborn joined. So the many graveyards of New England are poems.

Next, churches. Certainly the churches will be next in order of notice by the Western, younger American. They rise commonly from the gravestones. These, he will confess, are entirely fitting and beautiful. Even if only for their spires. Here, for once, New Englanders did not spare their pine; they sent it soaring to heaven in unbridled generosity. The Wren churches of London were never so graceful, so slender, so tender in shadows of mouldings and columns as these New World, Neo-Greek buildings. New England's white pine takes the Greek orders and architraves better than marble or brick. On almost every fifth hill there will be the inevitable slender spires. Plowmen orient their furrows by them. Lobstermen steer home by their whiteness. They lift up the housewife's mind and eyes. Along the sea, their vanes spell life or death. When the herring are running and the men are out, the eyes of women and children are often on that high white spire.

These churches, though many of them are often empty and

unused houses now, almost never go without white paint—the heraldic hue of New England, on boats, on barns, on houses. The farmers, who no longer attend church services much, would let their huge barns cry for paint before they would skimp on their churches. Their churches mean a good deal to them still. It may be, I swear, even more than they did when their grandfathers had to attend hour-long sermons there twice a Sunday and give a tithe of their tilth to support a "settled" minister. For what happened in old Greece is happening now in old New England: Religion is fading out as history and becoming a sense of proportion and a poetry of aspiration. A state of mind rather than a state of explicit grace. A symbol of the life taller than a man's, rather than Ten or even Twenty Commandments. And the beautifully proportioned and tall church is concrete reminder of man's looking above himself, a right thing to have on any hill.

In my young years, as a student at Oxford, I had the chance to read many fine definitions of religion in words of mediaeval Latin by men who lived their theology every waking and sleeping moment. I was reading John Donne's sermons; and as he often quoted the Church Fathers, I read them, too. There in the language of Augustine and Jerome, of Chrysostom and Ambrose, "men who have gold and honey in their names," as Donne describes them, I came on many metaphors full of honey and magic for religion. Yet I swear on my honor as a poet, I never, in any Church Father, came on any so powerful and apt or lovely a definition of what religion is all about as the one I saw, when a small boy in creaking new shoes, through the windows of a country church, on the green carpet of Summer Maine. Oh, I know I was risking my immortal soul, for it was a Baptist church, and I was a Congregationalist. But this church was the nearest one to our farm, and I went there. The church is still there, on the old road between Brunswick and Bath; it has a wonderfully American name that goes well with the green carpet, from its place—New Meadows Church. It was the pinnacle of my experience of religion so far, sitting in that church and looking out. And the color of that religion is green.

Country Church

He could not separate the thought
Of God from daisies white and hot
In blinding thousands by a road
Or dandelion disks that glowed
Like little suns upon the ground.
Holiness was like the sound
Of thousands of tumultuous bees
In full-blossomed apple trees,
Or it was smell of standing grain,
Or robins singing up a rain.

For the church he went to when
He was eight and nine and ten
And good friends with the trees and sun,
Was a small white country one.
The caraway's lace parasols
Brushed the clapboards of its walls,
The grass flowed round it east and west,
And one blind had a robin's nest.
Before the sermon was half over,
It turned to fragrance of red clover.

> May and June and other weather
> And farmers' wives came in together,
> At every window swung a bough,
> Always, far off, someone's cow
> Lowed and lowed at every pause.
> The rhythms of the mighty laws
> That keep men going, to their graves,
> Were no holier than the waves
> The wind made in the tasselled grass
> A small boy saw through window glass.

So the white country churches of New England are poems. These, too, are New England essences, and essentials of poetry.

Item: barns. These may not come exactly next in order of notice by an outsider; but I am sure the Westerner would very early be much impressed by these white or red or gray houses of New Englanders, larger often than our churches, into which each November of our years we all must take all our cattle and sheep and poultry, and all the green of the countryside we can. For man in this North must roll up his green carpet and take it in in the months of the death by snow. And in these warm houses are the tenderest beginnings of poems, in this act of making members of our family out of the beasts, taking in heifers and horses as one calls home his children. Often, north of Boston, these barns are attached to our houses; all of a piece with them. They loom so large to me that I shall devote a whole chapter to them. No Westerner who has been in one of these buildings in Winter, at the milking hour, but will know that here, too, is something that makes New England more than an act of geography;

makes it a charter of the brotherhood of creatures indeed, an art of humanity. So New England barns are poems.

Next, villages. This northern New England is villages. Small white groups of homes keeping close together, out of the wind and for company, keeping close to the church and the graveyard they feed. It is amazing to the Westerner how many of the people north of Boston live in white houses at a crossroads, by a village green. For the green carpet is where they look their best. They must band together around a grassy place to keep the wild pines and wild briars out, to keep looking into one another's eyes by day and into one another's windows at night. These villages are always neat, picked up, painted, to keep up good appearances against the background of decay; careful, to correct nature's carelessness; cheerful, against the crowding forest's sadness. The lights in the villages go out early, to save expense:

> The houses that are going dark
> Shelter ones who toe the mark
> Their ancestors learned how to toe
> Among long harvests of the snow
> And the short ones of the corn.
> These old friends of stone and thorn
> Are going to bed to save the light
> And letting neat birches have the night.

So many of the best men and women we have had started in these small white communities! Much of the most momentous history we have had so far is to be found, not in our wars or Faneuil Halls, town-halls or other places of legislature, or even our churches, but in these villages. In this we

march with men infinitely older than the Boys of '76; we
march with a mankind that does not change greatly through
the ages, or decay. So naturally we shall not go out of date or
out of literature. They bid us goodbye, every so often, but
back we come in our small villages:

> In the sound of peace and bees
> The houses stand by twos and threes
> Around a green quiet as time
> With railings small brown boys can climb;
> Each house is whiter than blown snow.
> Business was finished long ago
> In this place, one might suppose,
> Save for the grass blades, save for the rose.
>
> Clearly more people sleep alone
> On green beds headed by a stone,
> Their histories written at their heads,
> Than sleep in all the houses' beds.
> Write off this village. Close the book.
> But there is a brown cow with a hook
> To her horn and breath like silk
> Still giving milk, still giving milk.
>
> There are the little brown boys there
> With sun for hair, with light for hair,
> They will shoot up, first thing you know,
> As men. The boys will grow, will grow.
> And among them now and then
> Will be a Thoreau, Emerson,
> And people will have, sure as the rain,
> To open New England's ledger again.

The light and life will not go out in such villages so long
as straight devotio_ to life and belief in good neighbors and

good Samaritans last. Not all the group-civics of a thousand years to come will be able to obliterate the individuals who flourish here in these small communities of good friends. Any stage manager showing us the insides of such neighborly places, be they Grover's Corners in Thornton Wilder's *Our Town,* or Still Corners, or Merrymeeting Bay, will, as he explains these villages, grow gradually before our very eyes into the Stage Manager who sets out the stars for the whole world at night. (By the way, Wilder, this analyst of New Hampshire villagehood, is another major writer, in our time, at this late date for any New Englander to write, sprung from run-out New England soils. American literature will have to be reopened to take him in—and the world's.) So our small villages are poetry where time counts for nothing.

Along about now this Western observer of us must be beginning to believe that maybe the New England people, doing well with what little they have, whose motto is "Wear it out, use it up, make it do," are the most notable of all the features of the New England landscape, though he did not notice the people much at first, and are the reason why new poets keep coming up out of the north-of-Boston soil. These people were so quiet and untalkative, kept so much to themselves, kept their virtues so much out of sight—it is a New England custom—that the Westerner did not give them much thought. They did not advertise their attractions or their agonies; they did not wear their hearts on their sleeves, or roll up their shirts to show where they had been hard-hit, as so many modern writers in Russia do. So our visitor made the mistake that so many other students of us have made these last years. To hear New Englanders talk about the weather or the Democrats and the New Deal that deals all the cards off the bottom of the deck, the observer gets to thinking that no one hereabouts is hard-hit ever, the people seem so light on their feet and in their wit. And that is where he is wrong, for we have been hit harder by economic change and the change in *mores* and the deadly drift towards false ideals of security than most regions of the earth, since it was largely our ideals of security that have been supplanted by the false beacons set up by demagogues. But few observers ever *are* able to see the shadow and the tragedy in New England for the brightness of our scenery and the bright sparkle of New England minds.

Make no mistake, though, this bright-eyed Westerner newly among us does find enough that is colorfully and typically American, too, about these north-of-Boston, small-village people. He finds the older and more lasting and more poetic patterns especially. Pioneer patterns, because they were good and enduring patterns and not because we were backward as Toynbee suggests, still flourish in abundance. It is all the more surprising to find pioneering still going on strong in these houses so well finished at the eaves, so urban and Georgian in their architecture, so well proportioned in their finish and cupolas, in fireplaces and front-doors. Georgian architecture, yet New World downrights inside the houses.

One of these pioneer patterns is making much of our children. That is a surviving older American custom still in the New England far enough north of Boston to be out of the shadow of Harvard University. We Americans, the British say, have the best-dressed and worst-behaved children in the world. There is something of truth in this. We cannot help spoiling our children sometimes, here and there, we regard them so highly, as something very precious, as the older Missourians did. It goes back to a time when children, along with our cattle, were our only estate. When children mean a future nation or our best hope of an improved world, we are bound to take them into the family firm even in babyhood, and make them the center of all our life. My father did that with us ten boys and girls. He let us go in boats and buggies and help him long before we could talk. He let us pass him shingle nails on roofs, even when we were young enough to put some of them into our mouths and swallow them; he let us help him build a house before we could reason very well. It was good for him and us. New England people center their affections in children. They take them into partnership early. They let them sit up all hours. It is one of the prime virtues of New England:

Coast Babies Sit Up Late

Coast babies sit up very late at night,
They have an oar in all the family plans,
The father makes allowance for their eyes
As he makes allowance for a man's.

His son may be too young to say a word,
His daughter so new she smiles and nothing more,
But the coast man loves to have a young
Center to work around upon his floor.

He likes to have a pair of bright eyes watch
When he splices rope or mends a trawl,
He gravely asks approval and advice
Of one who does no more than clap or crawl.

[153]

He asks the baby how the wind will turn,
And answers for him and agrees he's right,
He gets a dozen things much better done,
Having so bright a center to his night.

When the baby's head leans over at last,.
The man puts out his huge and gnarled and red
Tender hands and gently, gently takes
The center of the universe to bed.

So even New England babies are the beginnings of new poems.

Somewhere along his observing way the Westerner will be struck with the areas of woodland in this New England. The land is darker than it was in Whittier's day. The forests are growing; they are putting out the lights in more and more mountain farmhouses year by year. There are fewer farms by one-half now north of Boston than there were fifty years ago. The many young men who strung the mountains with thousands of miles of stonewalls are gone now from shrunken family circles. The young often move away from the shrinking meadows and enlarging and lonely houses. The outsider begins to get the sad and disturbing impression that this is a land of old men. He sees mostly old people, spading the dwindled garden, pitching the dwindled hay. The wild is coming back. Year by year it gains on man and his works. It swallows up his cultivated acres, his house, his very grave. It is sad for the few sons of those who tamed this land to see it return to forest. It is, perhaps, the leading New England tragedy. Trees that should feed children feed the wild things. Land that once fed the tame feeds the wild.

The New England Green

The Woodland Orchard

These apple trees were lost for good
When the little house which stood
Nearby to keep them safe and sound
Sank moldering into the ground
And the children went away.
The waiting forest won the day,
And came and took the orphaned trees
Upon its dark and kindly knees.

The sun comes down more golden here
Than it comes ever in the clear;
The grass is greener for the wall
Of the forest round it all,
There are no feet to tramp it down,
Except the little ones in brown
Beneath a deer that comes to stand
And wonder at this tame, sweet land.

You might say this was a spot
Where tame and wild for once forgot
Their old hate; the partridge feeds
On fruit sprung of men's tended seeds
And pecks the apples touched by frost.
But these are trees that have been lost;
Here one draws a careful breath,
This loveliness is so like death.

Yet these people who are saddened to see the woods return
are New Englanders. They have acquired the New England
wisdom of making the most of what little is left. They make
the most of the tall green enemies that have invaded their
happy green pastures. After all, these trees and the slim deer

they hide are New Englanders, too. They belong here, they have a right to come if people thin out and move away. The new New Englanders have discovered there is justice and good neighborliness, a good life to believe in, even in the deep woods:

Out of Mind

Go light, hold breath,
Here lie men lost
To the careless forgetters,
The forest, the frost.

Here lie golden children
Lost to the sun,
Two-footed beauty
To four-footed one.

Tremulous deer
Powdered with pearls
Have usurped the slimness
Of little girls.

The sole mothers here
Have paws, wear wings,
There are no words
To the songs love sings.

The white houses fell
Into the ground,
White birches pay calls
With no motion, no sound.

The ferns and the firs
Are friends and caress,
In small rabbits still
There is tenderness.

The New England Green

But the love still here
Is not our kind,
Go quickly, men are
Out of sight and mind.

We in New England are beginning to learn to forgive the
forest its green trespasses. We are becoming charitable to a
wider circle of neighbors than the older New Englanders
knew, these last two centuries. We are becoming believers
in a wider brotherhood in forgiving the deer for coming back
where they belong, in our gardens and our lives. So even the
woods are becoming poems, good poems of community.

In all ways then, little by little, deeper and deeper, the
western student of New England comes upon that last and
best of the virtues that are New England, and will be New
England, I hope, centuries to come. It is the togetherness of
things: The togetherness of the living and the dead, the
houses and the barns, the churches and the green pastures
and plowed fields, the togetherness of children and old ones,
togetherness of mountains and lakes and valleys, of the land
and the sea, of hard, long Winters and quick brief Summers,
of apocalyptic Autumns and plain humble people, the togetherness of small villages and great thoughts, of solitude
and close neighborliness, of the deer and trees and men. All
these togethernesses everywhere point like golden vanes towards the prevailing poems, written and unwritten—Oh,
voluminously unwritten still!—in this paradox of a tilted-up,
serene, fertile, infertile, lonely, companionable, sweet and
salt, bitterly beautiful land.

These are the poems of New England's old and enduring
good health. *Community:* The New England people, who,

[157]

when all is said and done, are New England's richest crop, have learned to fit well into their place. Better than most people, anywhere. And it isn't solely because they have been here so long a time; there's more of a fundamental charity to the phenomenon.

These people have fitted the contours of their bodies and the configurations of their minds into the mountains, into their strong winds from the sea and the Arctic, into their forests, their small houses and vast barns and high churches, into the multitudinous rocks in their soil, the sharp angles of their weather, the tides they know and the eternities of their sea. They belong. And as people who belong so to a carpet perpetually green, they belong in literature, in poetry. And these people will likely be here for the purposes of poetry for a long time to come. There are harvests in New England still to be gleaned that are richer than any of the starry ones Emerson dreamed. For they are a tender green and all of one piece with Shakespeare's countryside, with his countrified kings and queens. They are the good green poems, wide as Virgil and Shakespeare and Herrick and the world. Thoreau did no more than make a mere beginning of bringing them in, in his living close to green woods in Concord and to green spruces and mountains of Maine.

As long as the geography of New England remains what it is, and the New England weather endures as the bright, hard whetstone it is, and as long as some people of old or new stocks inhabit that place and learn to get along in it, as my own northern people have learned, so long will New England not want for poetry. The green carpets of its hills and woods and the blue and green carpets of its sea are good

The New England Green

reeders and makers of good men and women and good
oems. New Englanders will always be people of symmetry;
eople the better for the touch of sadness always on them.
have tried to put my New England people into words. The
oem is about a particular New England island, with a
aunt name so typical of our islands' contours, Ragged. It is
he island that happened just now to belong to the greatest
voman poet this side of Sappho, who, I am proud to say, was
Maine human being, Edna St. Vincent Millay. Yet many
ther islands of the Maine coast world would do as well to
onvince our western visitor finally that a small and hard
nd often lonely region may breed hard and handsome men.

This Is My Country

This is my country, bitter as the sea,
Pungent with the fir and bayberry.
An island meadow, stonewalled, high, and lost,
With August cranberries touched red by frost.
Two hours of sun before the fog erases
The walls on walls of trees trimmed sharp as laces.
A house behind the last hill of them all,
And, after that, the lonesome seagulls' call;
A juniper upon a windy ledge,
Splendor of granite on the world's bright edge,
A heron on the beach and one on wing,
Wind wrapped round each last and living thing,
A lighthouse like a diamond, cut and sharp,
And all the trees like strings upon a harp.

These are my people, saving of emotion,
With their eyes dipped in the Winter ocean,
The lonely, patient ones, whose speech comes slow,

On the Green Carpet

Whose bodies always lean towards the blow,
The enduring and the clean, the tough and clear,
Who live where Winter is the word for year
And the briar rose had best be brief,
Where most trees wear a dagger for a leaf.
These people are my kindred and my kind,
They have a sort of lighthouse for a mind,
Keeping lit inside, because the sun
Is too low to be a trusted one,
The cheerful, crystal people who have had
The chance to know the taste of being sad.

V

GREEN MAINE

5. *Green Maine*

The green carpet is wide. The poet at his strongest is small. He is the singer of the delicate, definite part. He is the man of metonymy. The part must represent the whole but in quick, sharp particulars. For poetry is, first, last, and always, metonymy. So let me look homeward today, go nearer and still nearer home. From all the up-and-down green carpet of northern New England, I must choose my own piece.

I have a formula for the lyric poem. It is the process of narrowing in. The poet grows exactly in ratio to his confining himself and his setting. He grows through the provincialization of his emotions. So my formula runs, for me, thus: Maine is the most poetic of the northeastern states. But there are two Maines, the island and coastal; the Maine that is woods and lakes and mountains; the Maine that is woods and mountains and sea. I must choose one. My Maine is the Maine of the sea. The other is not worth its salt. But the Maine seacoast is a long and varied one; it runs, measured along the edge of high tide, nearly three thousand miles. That is too long for a poet. There are scores of great bays; I must select one. I choose Casco Bay. Yet Casco Bay has over two hundred islands in it, and several scores of handsome smaller bays. I must draw in. I take Harpswell as my part of my bay. But there are two Harpswells: the Neck and its open fields; and the other eastern, island half with its forests of pointed cedars and laces of firs and spruces bearded with age. The wild island Harpswell shall be mine. And that is where I grew up and grew poetic, anyway. Yet there are too many islands here. So I choose my own Sebascodegan as mine. And yet this one island is serrated with too many lovely coves and harbors. I will select its northwestern spine, the peninsula of my father, Lost Paradise Farm. Still, when I come to write of this farm I lived on, certain hills and harbors of it, Apple Tree Cove, Lower Oak Landing, and Dragonfly Spring, stand out above all the rest. So, finally, I have come to my one dedicated greenest glade, under the ledge where columbines rang their silent gold-throated red bells in the west wind, lady slippers floated like independent, airy hearts under the pines, and a heron with powder of stars around his eyes stood, taller than I was, by a pool with the live emeralds of crabs in it, still as time. Concentration is consecration. I have put metonymy into practice. I have gone inward, gone homeward, come into my own. I am ready, now, to sing. Of course, I have gone into hyperbole in my illustration here, gone too far to prove my point. Yet one of the powers of poetry is going too far. And there is wisdom and justice behind my formula.

Hence I take Maine now, and particularly my coastal, crystal half of Maine, as my best means of proving my whole thesis of the regenerative and transfiguring power of the green carpet. Remember, by the words of that children's folksong, we must choose a true-love, the one thing we love the best, to illustrate all things, to represent all true love. So I choose Maine, my own part of upper New England, to stand

best for the best of all that grows on the green north of
Boston.

I think, too, that I am wise in my choice. For the green
carpet that is Maine has been least changed by the process
called progress, least invaded and discolored by cities and the
urban mind. Its people are still chiefly country people; and
its people have "stayed put," as the colorful and exact colloquial phrase is; they, in their ancestors, have been here a
long time. They have had a chance to learn what there is to
learn, from the skies and the sharp sweetfern, bayberries and
briars, and the angular humanity of their place.

Now there is an amazing plenty! An endless variety is
another metaphor for Maine. Yet all that variety has learned
to look well together. If metonymy is plucking the heart
from the whole, taking the essential, it is also a brave attempt
to conceive of several vast wholes together. Togetherness! It
is the word for Maine, surely. It is also the word for poetry.
Togetherness means cousinship, consanguinity; and these are
other names for poetry, I believe. If that is so, then Maine is
the state of being in a state of poetry. The makings of poems
shine and show everywhere, just as the delicate flutings of
shells of mussels and crabs which spread white lace around
all the pasture ledges testify to the poetry and presence of the
sea. A man can hardly take a step without having a poem, a
compounded metaphor, under his foot. For when he walks
this high coast, since the sea seems to lean forever uphill, he
has under his upraised sole a cubistic harbor with ivory cubes
for houses or the white thorn of a lighthouse. His next step
may crush a clean pod of a sailboat or startle Lilliputians in a
white village the size of a patch of white woodland violets.

[167]

I have made poems of this up-and-down concentration of crystals which is the near-far handsomeness of Maine.

This togetherness, this closeness of wide loveliness, in my corner of New England ranges through the topography, the weather, the fauna and flora, the history, the houses and the human beings who live in this dark-bright place.

For our darkness and light do come fiercely side by side. Down a vista more skylike than sky you stare into the midnight of a balsam island. Black Spanish lace of spruces borders and closes the azures of all bays; it is behind all milk-white houses, it runs below all light blues of distant mountains. The rocks have stars in them; granite makes all ancient peninsulas seem new at their edges. The enamelled lustre of pine needles and spruce spills makes the days shine like green glass. The sparkle of fairweather waves in the long sun, as I like to say, is like the rolling downhill of cut diamonds. One comes around an old mountain, and comes on a world still dewy as it was the first Monday of Creation. Capes shine with snowsqualls in Winter, with gull-squalls in Summer. Winters and Summers are the same bright cloth, a brocade of silks and beads. Years bring no sobering to these shouting colors and crying translucencies. It is all like glass. Time cannot fade these clean farmhouses or this freshness on all things. Everything glitters, everything shines. Lighthouses shine, boats gleam, pines run like molten silver in the gales. Like landscape, like people. The lobstermen shine, too, standing stiff in their dories like bronze. Another name for Maine, besides metaphor, is light.

Maine is mostly mountains. Yet the mountains of the interior grow lonely and lonesome from not being looked at much; the mountains guess there is something more beautiful than themselves that is being looked at down to the east and south; they have caught glimpses of it far away. So the mountains march down to the sea themselves, they march up the side of the sea, so they, too, will be looked at and admired. Vast forests we have still; yet they also tire of being by themselves, and down they troop to the seacoast, and up they climb on all the islands until all our islands are floating forests. Our little villages climb down the cliffs; our churches wander into the woods and outshine the white birches there which gleam on the dark green. Roads lean on headlands steeply down to get below the gulls. Deer come into our pastures to graze with our cows; our cows play truant in the woods and feed where slim foxes shine in the sudden sun.

It is the ideal place for a poet to be. He has little to do but set poems down as they come, green and gold and blue and quick on him, fresh and whole, clean as crystal, at every turn of the road, at every lift of the prow, at every turn of the tide.

This Is the Poem

This is the poem, this is Maine:
Sunlight on all things like frost,
Eternity at the end of the lane,
A garden deer have always crossed.

Woods that come down to the waves,
Pine boughs brushing the apple tree,
Cool white houses, high white graves,
And a man rowing up the sea.

Sweetfern growing in the corn,
The mountain on the whitecapped tide,

On the Green Carpet

A buck that feeds with slender horn
By the lamb's white gentle side.

The silver fish under the floor,
Lamps and lighthouses at night,
The secret and the sudden door
That opens dark in a hill of light.

Hot spruces and cool mussel shells,
Tame and friendly bells in under
Necks of cows and the wild bells
Rung by waves white with sea thunder.

A coast like columns fluted clean
Where common men like winged things go
Single forever, on paths that lean
Under a sky alive with snow.

Seasons of the year, in Maine, have this same togetherness. The frost comes, bluish white beside the light-blue frost-flowers. That final flower of our year is a natural metaphor and an instance of this togetherness at once. Winter returns on a March afternoon and hangs the willows with larger pussywillows than those of Spring. March gales blow open July's first wild roses on the headlands; and the sea is snowed with living snowflakes. Summers come back in wistful Indian Summers of November. Trees become trees of a second blossoming; and all the Summer's radiance comes out in light on them just at the edge of snow. July splendor burns on the iced landscape of January. Nights burn with Northern Lights. Evenings bring in a second, brighter day in golden afterglow.

It is the same with history. The togetherness of different times is a fact on every hand. Men still bank their houses in Winter with evergreens as the Indians did theirs; they plant the corn in Indian hills on a fat alewife. The oxen of the *Bible* still strain to the yoke and draw timber out in the swamp. Boats are built as the Indians built theirs, high in the stem and stern. We gather the sweet blood of maples when the sun is low in the low year as the Indians did. We make today's reach-boat in the same harbor where vast schooners and ships were built, out of the same oak and pine. The past is not the past; the present is not the present, but worshipful work by hand. Hunters go Indian and read the books of winds and running water. We sleep on the heaven of fir-balsam boughs as the Dawn People did ten thousand years ago. There are still many one-room schoolhouses bulging with boys and girls, with dogs waiting on the doorstep.

The same with houses. They fit into the ledges and the winds. We slant the roofs that fend off the cold blows in the lee of spruces that keep off the north wind; our windows let in all the light of the south and east they can. Our houses and doors look to sea and lobster traps and boats and life there. We orient our beds to the rising sun, or point them to the Pole. We take the shortest way to the well and pantry that our grandmothers worked out for us. We are begotten and die in the same rooms of the generations of men. We and the past are one indivisible, one whole enduring cloth, wool, and a yard wide; and the future is sure.

Men show the same togetherness of substances and certainties. They seem to have no one calling. A good lobsterman makes good hay, and a hoer of turnips is also a hoer of

[171]

clams and quahaugs. Farmers are hunters and lumbermen; fishermen are carpenters and masons. The trades run together. The herring-catcher reads books. Carpenters are engineers; engineers, plumbers and painters. A steep Maine farm calls out a dozen skills in one man; a small Maine kitchen, many provinces in the same woman. We use machinery when we can, when we can afford it, but our rocky farms are too small and steep often for any but hand-work. Men marry the dories they have made; and a new centaur-like breed, half man, half boat, runs on the waves out towards Fundy. Little boys often row before they can walk very well. A keel is man's extended feet out on the bronze mountains of the Gulf of Maine. Children learn to walk with high ocean winds to lean on. Fishermen go with the sea forever in their bending knees. Happiness and hard work come close together; it is hard for a freckled sunburnt boy to tell where work leaves off and play begins. Men make work play. A farmer's small son makes a most sober business of coasting down his long farm all a Winter's day and out upon the sea.

Our farms are amphibian. Cows learn to navigate in fogs. Horses become good sailors, going over the ocean to town in a gun-low. Red astrakhans shine through the slats of a clam-basket, and a last-year dory blossoms out, not with little honey-haired girls out fishing on the ocean with their father, but with red geraniums in the back dooryard. Nets shine not solely with smelts but also with daisies where they stretch over half the world of green grass after their tarring. Fogs and foggy sheep hug the headlands together. Side by side, wild and tame; bell-buoys and cowbells weave together their high and low music into one lovely sound. I do not know of

[172]

another place on earth where you can see this poem happen:
A brown boy with tangled sunlight on his head for hair is
coming home on a tanned load of hay, and his brother—his
twin brother—with the same sunny hair and blue eyes, is
coming home alongside him, only a few rods away, sprawled
out on the deck of their father's boat; one by blue and one by
gold; one on land and one on water. So together things here
can be.

I know a number of the coasts of our world, but not one
so much a congress of them all as Maine's. The wildness of
Morocco, the highness of Norway and Spain, the wooded
glooms of Norway and the bareness of Brittany, the close-
cropped emerald turf of Cornwall, Cornwall's sadness and
Scotland's gaiety, the deep estuaries of Norway, the cliffs of
Devon and the rocks of Brittany, and the lost, God-forsaken
mountains that break off sheer in the sea of North Wales—
Maine is all these. Cliffs and harbors, gulfs and woods,
beaches and bluffs, houses and high ospreys—all together,
side by side, over and under, far and near, *ultimae Thules*
and cheery small houses with urban radio music in them.

Nowhere else on the world will you find these poems of
togetherness which are Maine. Nowhere else such marriages
of sea and land, sky and trees, people and weather. Here is
the only coast of the world where the long green leaves of the
corn dip in the ocean at high-run tide. Here is the only shore
where red clover comes right down to the marsh-rosemary
and rockweed. Farmers trip and turn their plows on a
pebbly beach, wheel their horses and go back up their garden
rows which lean to the sea. Hot small boys step out of blue
overalls and plunge into cold ocean foam at each bean-row's

lower end. Boatfuls of silver herring come home level with loads of silver birchwood on carts. A sailboat comes walking the high woods. And over orchards in full blow blooms the whole white-capped Atlantic. The smell of hot pine and blueberries mingles with the cold smell of kelp and waves on a burning hot Summer's day. The cries of new-born lambs and infant plovers are braided all together. Voices of men and the mourning of seagulls. High and low, near and far. White gulls and white sheep; blue morning-glories above blue mussel shells. To be in such a place, all the bright and dark days of the year, is to be a poet.

Maine is metaphor. No one could possibly keep from mingling birds and boats here, endurance with eagles, hope with harbors, and solitude and cliffs with sadness and strength. Lighthouses stand on the ragged edges of earth and teach good neighborliness night after night, year after year, lifetime after lifetime. Sudden safe harbors in the escarpments of a windy chaos preach Providence; and generosity is taught in every man's front dooryard by quahaugs and clams. A light at a window by a lonely bay becomes an argument for eternity. Charity blues the world with unplanted blueberries, and reddens it with wild raspberries and strawberries. Men bound home can smell home in a deep fog because home is meadows filled with wild strawberries. Men living under mountains grow to be like mountains; men long in the winds color like the winds and steady and straighten in their bodies. Light gets into a man's brain and looks out bright blue at his deep eyes. Winds get into the hollows of the agile mackereler's bones. Sails get into a man's manners and gestures; he goes slowly with a high grace upon him.

[174]

Green Maine

At every bend in a coast all bays a metonymy waits. An osprey takes upon himself all the life and magic of motion; a single breaker on a beach is man's slow, masculine delay in his deepest emotions. A single house becomes security, a lone spar-buoy, vigilance. An oaken rib in a hull is all strength. A change of wind means life or death. The shining part argues the shining whole. One poem of a sunset sums up the long serenity of a lifetime. The vast one is seen in one woman standing with a lantern against a dark night to guide her mate in his dark dory into his cove. The part proves the whole. The one heartbeat the history of life.

Here on this metaphor of a seacoast, all beauty is doubled, all sadness and solitude darken twice. Goods come paired; and woes make common cause with the wind.

Here at the azure corner of the world
Sweet fields come down to meadows of the sea,
Red clovers dip their flowers in high water,
White houses and white sails keep company.
No cowbell rings so lonely but there is
A bell that answers it upon the waves,
A hollow bell rung lonesome by the tide
Tolls above the schooners' shadowy graves.
The hayrack and the boat go side by side,
Level, on earth and sea, small brothers ride.

Every good and sorrowful thing comes double:
Blue herons and morning-glories bring up dawn,
Blue shells of wild-pea fringe the mussel-bed,
Bleached clamshells shine by daisies on the lawn.
When the strong man bows his iron head
On his empty arms at night and grieves,
A strong wind from the ocean will arise

[175]

And come and mourn with him around the eaves.
When wives sit still with sorrow in their eyes,
High over all the world the seagull cries.

This continuous metaphor of Maine breeds brotherhood. Make no mistake about that. The flow of splendid detail is not lost motion. It moves, like the flood-tide itself, to a moving plentitude; it moves towards life. These sparkling and small bright tangibles, as the golden motes of dust in a beam of light in a dark forest or barn prove the existence of a sun, prove a source of all motion and being.

A small symmetrical high-nosed dory goes up the long hill of the sea. It bobs under mountains. It is full of sharp particulars of sea-harvest, antennaed lobsters and thorny crabs, living shears, dark green and rankling with particular hate and hunger. The tall, long-visored lobsterman leans forward and strokes with flashing oars catching the lift of each swell. He, too, is of his own kind, himself, no other like him there on half a skyful of land-mountains and sea-mountains. He and his boat are all there is of the particular. Yet he and his boat are enough to prove and point up all that vast, those two infinities of splendid ocean and sky, blue sea, blue sky, blue mountains; the man makes the infinities tangible and really their vast selves. He gives scale. Now the blue deserts become alive, they lean in on that man; he meets and masters those great leaners and goes on his particular way to his lobster buoys, homely little points in eternity. The leaners draw back and leave the man alone, and they are proud and give thanks. For his being proves theirs.

An island can do as much for a man. It can wall him about with solitude and make him more warmly and particularly a man. He will sing at his work and work better for being alone. An ocean fog can play the part of infinity, too. It can come up, from nothing, from a small wraith on a Summer's morning; and in ten minutes it can wash away the man's world of hills and islands and harbors brightly seen and steered by into mystery, a fable, a nothing. And alone, the man must set up his own headlands to go by in his own head, he must become a whole distant coast himself, the pin-prick of a cove, his own salvation, and go straight home into himself. It is a revelation to any man to have to do that, so quickly, without warning, on a Summer's day. And the necessity makes a better man of him.

Being in Maine, clearly, is being close to the vast, becoming a neighbor to eternity.

And all this is because of the presence of that shapeless shaper of men through their long history, the sea. The sea has always been our greatest civilizer even more than cities, which are the offspring of the sea. The sea built Crete's palaces and passions, the temples and civics of Athens, London's independence and thrift. Maine with its deeply indented coast, long mountains of peninsulas, and schools of bright islands resembles Greece and its archipelagoes very closely. And something of the art of being itself, its own arbiter, its own destiny, makes independent Maine, the metaphor of coasts, into a metonymy not unlike the continual poem that was Athens. The sea that was anciently and always in our Anglo-Saxon blood through centuries of European living shines in Maine like a promised and perpetual homeland to us.

When the good green carpet with its colors and textures

of eternity comes down the hills and joins the eternity and creative urges which are the ocean, then the whole sphere of our being widens out into the limitlessness of poetry, and everyday living becomes poem on poem. So it seems to me.

It does something to a man, certainly, to live beside the infinite. With twice as many and as strong winds to blow him clear and clean as the country man, the landsman, has, he grows clearer and cleaner. Put even the homeliest man, I am fond of saying, out in the coast winds and suns for fifty years, and then go and look for him. He will not be there. But a handsome man will be. The man will have grown into something so like the clouds and sky that he will melt into them and be lost; and you will have to admit there are only handsome men here, none but comely cosmic men. It is a formula the world could well follow. And many of our coasts, in these years of crowding into the cities, are untenanted and bare.

It is good for a man to know there is, at his boots' ends, a place he can never wholly possess, always more than he is, and less, mystery and unshaped and unshapable power. Something vast and strange and superior. Such a thing is the sea. It rolls and is alive there; it makes us humble, makes us believe more fearfully in ourselves. It is the line we cannot ever step over, any more than could King Canute.

Here Ends Desire

The furrow ends in the white birds,
There are no houses, are no words
Any more beyond that blue
The little farm runs up into.

Green Maine

The rippling corn knows this is all,
The last sweet cascades of it fall
Over and touch the stars of salt,
The living ladders of wild vetch halt.

The thorny bronze wild-briar knows
And opens its last and sweetest rose
On the azure otherwhere
Where no bush will ever bear.

The youngest, friskiest ram-lamb gazes
Into a silence that amazes
And sees life there is only wings,
Not running warm and woolly things.

The bronze small boy stares into the end,
There is no love, there is no friend
To follow farther into that bright
Conclusion more complete than night.

The old pines lean with turned-back boughs,
Here ends desire, peace, and plows,
The late last house hangs on the hill,
The rest is sea and strange and still.

It is an image of the first stirrings that mountained up all life
out of the dust of chaos. The sea, mother of the first gods,
the place—the only place—where godhead now might seem
to many to be:

Unfinished End of the World

Something terrible and good was there,
Trees leaned away from it with fearful boughs,
White houses hid from its presence everywhere,
And all tame meadows wrinkled by old plows.

On the Green Carpet

It was as though someone had left a door
Open on holy uncompleted things,
From that creating chaos there would pour
Hourly waste beauty and wild wings.

Birds flew from that unfinished end of the world,
Unbroken to the economies of earth,
Too sharp for trees were the pinions they uncurled,
Too much like sorrow were their cries of mirth.

Winds, the only lawless creatures left,
Came from the undetermined power there,
They leaned upon the land their godlike heft
And troubled with gods' voices the high air.

That wistful, blue and wilful empty place
Was where the only gods this late could be;
All trees, all houses, minds of men, all peace
Leaned away from it. It was the sea.

Where the two carpets, the green and the blue, meet, men's houses become comelier. Brighter for the salt in the winds, more weathered with the weather, the homes of New England grow finer as they come nearer the ocean. This is especially so in Maine. The architecture takes shapeliness from the boats, both the vast sailing vessels of a century ago and from the fishing boats now. It is another example of togetherness. But it is more than a matter of houses putting on the best appearances in the face of infinity. Something of that vastness at their front doors comes into the houses themselves; rooms grow larger without growing, for having the surf of white daisies and the meadows of whitecaps at all their small panes; a twelve-foot room grows in the sea-light into a large place where old people sit with eyes accustomed to far-seeing and the coming of good news or sad news from the sea.

Men's Sunday houses grow in loveliness, too. There are no churches on the world quite so good-looking as the white ones that serve as lighthouses to fishing men returning by day from trouble, chance, and hard work. Not only is there the carpet of green fields through the windows but the ocean's green pastures as well. And maybe sweet water will come past the windows to join the salt. Religion keeps young in such a house opening its windows upon two eternities.

Church on Water

Always in music, nights and days and years,
Will this small church by the river be,
Where the green water curves over the cliffs
And goes down white and steep into the sea.

Never, to sing the old Creator's praise,
Will this house be without young congregations,
For, all the Aprils, teeming alewives come
Climbing these singing falls in their white nations.

So lucky the people are who worship here
Beside the running children old as dawn,
Waters going to sea and fish to land,
Children the years can put no weariness on.

Men and women in this happy house
Can look out from good faces and good words
And see good winds and waters going by,
Blue herons and white seagulls, the clean birds.

[181]

It should be easy to believe between
Organs of falling waters and the sea,
Here feet and fins and wings are cousinly,
Time is the small brother to eternity.

The spire of the church, tallest point of many coast villages, bears the apt iconography of the weather vane; and men consult that clean arrow of the vane daily. For if they put out in their boats when the wind is backing around the compass, when that arrow points the wrong way, the men will not come home. The coast church has fitted itself into daily life, and death.

The plowman sent his little boy to see
If wind stood in a quarter that was fair,
And many a woman looked up to the church,
With men off on the sea, as though at prayer.

The lobstering man said, "Sonny, run and look
How she stands." The small boy, out of breath,
Came shouting shrill, "She's backing round no'theast!"
And saved his sire a forty-fathom death.

Where the blue and the green carpets join, harvests are double. The silver of shad, the gold of the corn. Men come home from harvest in strange ways. A door in a floor opens, and up comes a man with starlight still on him by stairs from a boat bobbing on dark water. Houses as well as gardens hang over the tide. The herring school in lamplight through a window. Plain turnips and cabbages come over water and so take something vast into their flavor.

Green Maine

I think that the gathering of apples and the bringing of apples home is one of the best poems ever to shine on the green carpet. Apples, cousins of the sun—daughters of the rose, too, as botanists tell us—save all Summer and bring it home to houses just as frost spreads its starry death over the earth. But often, on the edge of the blue carpet, men's apples come home across an arm of the sea. And that makes a great poetic difference.

It was so on our saltwater farm years ago. My father had several tame apple orchards. He was always setting tame apples out. But the orchard I remember the best was a wild one. The trees were ancient. Their trunks were gnarled beyond belief, like those in fairybooks. They were covered with the cuneiform of woodpeckers and yellowhammers. People said the old Indians had planted the trees. Some of them were hollow-hearted, but the old shells still sprouted boughs of fruit. Some trees were prone, but apples still came out on them. Partridge fed in them under the October moon. The deer took fruit from their knotted boughs. Their tough twigs had turned hard as thorns. The fruit was hard as time, and small. When we boys bit into them, the apples bit us back. They were incredibly sour. But my father liked to have a few of these wild apples to point up the family's jelly and pies and cider. The wild often goes into the best Maine cooking. So my father gathered one day's harvest from these ancient apple trees. The orchard was at the far end of our island farm. There was no road up there. So we had to bring the apples home by boat. That made all the difference. Any boy could tell instantly something fine was going on. A poem

[183]

lovely enough in itself was being deepened and doubled. Any boy could tell he was taking part in a poem when apples were being brought home on an October day over the sea.

Apples by Ocean

Common sons and common fathers gathered
And brought tame apples home in blue-wheeled carts,
But this son and his father went by ocean
And rowed wild apples home through sapphires' hearts.

They carried sacks bulging with wild hard honey
From trees sown by thin Indians and deer,
Carried wild apples on their backs to the bayside
Through the cool bonfire of the dying year.

The smell of frost, the smell of briefened sunlight,
Of bayberry and apples mingled in,
The golden powder of the late light dusted
The man and boy on forehead, cheeks, and chin.

They walked through fiery dust up to their nostrils
And came bent low with apples to the shore,
Put down the bags in a boat spiced by salt water,
And pushed off into the ocean's azure core.

They sang past islands carved like polished onyx,
Their oars kept time in rhythm clear and sweet,
The scent of apples crushed in the sea water
Was sharp as sudden joy around their feet.

The evening over them was all clear amber,
They rowed unweary inside an amber stone
Electric with the light, the father being
A boy again, the boy a man full-blown.

[184]

Green Maine

They rowed home fast, but they knew they would never
Be home from sea or out of this golden night,
They would be with apples there forever
Walled in the immortality of light.

And what I say here is no soft fancy. It is hard as amber,
hard as steel. What I say here is so: My father is more alive to
me now in the light of a remembered October glow long
ago than he ever was in any actual glow of a real October. In
the smell of apples my father has eluded death, and he is
warm beside me now from his becoming a part of the sunset,
sunlit apples, and a part of the sea. Metonymy and metaphor,
really right there around me that evening long ago, for my
later poem's sake, have made my father immortal. Poems, I
swear, exist. They surely do in azure and amber Maine.

As with harvests, so with the harvesters. The poetic people
of the windrow and furrow, of the barn, the forest and
orchard, grow doubly poetic from the downward and upward light from the waves. Farmers grow wider for tides,
more friendly for lighthouses, more graceful for their agile
boats and the casting of nets. The man in men comes out
plainer; the woman in women. The old distances and distinctions between the sexes—lost now to the world, to the world's
mischief—reappear. Indoors, the wife; outdoors, the man.

The first thing a Maine man does when he goes into his
house is to shrink up three sizes instantly. His hands become
of a sudden too big for him and get in his way. He looks at
them surprised, they hang down on him like anchors. His
body bothers him. The clarity of his mind is clouded. He
keeps pretty quiet. He does not dare to interrupt the nice flow
of the routines of cookstove and dishes and his wife's talk.

He becomes a small boy. And all this is as it should be, for a man *should* take a lower seat in a house. It is the law. But outdoors it is just the other way. The man grows, the woman shrinks. The man goes ahead on the path, where a man should go. He heads out ahead of the woman in the strong wind and hard places and faces in advance into the vast. This also is the law. My test of a right poetic—and civilized—place, when I go to a new one, is to watch and see if the man take the lead of his woman when they are outdoors together. They are never together, the man is ahead. If he is, all is well, the place is poetic and civilized.

I know there are two schools of thought on this matter, even in Maine. One school—it can be called the Chivalric, I suppose—say that Maine coast men walk in advance of their wives because most of the Maine coast paths are narrow and steep, and they are forever bordered by sweetfern and hardhack, juniper and bayberry. And there is always water there on the path, beads of fog, drops of dew, drops of rain. So the men chivalrously goes ahead of his woman and brushes the drops off on his trousers so she will not get them on her skirt. That is all nonsense. I don't hold with that theory at all. There is no truth in the Chivalric School. The man goes in front because that is the right place for him to go. It was so in the time of Noah and Abraham; it will be so to the end of men's time. Outdoors, the man ahead.

The Race

When Harpswell children go to school,
The boys hang back of the girls to fool
In the frog-ponds and the ditches
And shin up trees and burst their stitches.

Green Maine

Later on, the tall young men
Catch up with the girls, and then
They walk level, side by side,
And folks get ready for a bride.

But three years more, young husbands go
Three paces on ahead or so
Among the junipers and boulders
And talk to their women over their shoulders.

Wife hurries up, her male and master
Hurries up just that much faster,
And all the world the woman eyes
Lies each side of her husband's thighs.

When the man is out ahead
Ten paces, then the man's been wed
Fifteen years, or maybe twenty,
Anyway, a pretty plenty.

Most of the seasoned husbands walk
So far ahead there is no talk
Between the pair, it takes a might
Of walking, keeping the man in sight.

Yet when the woman's hair is gray,
There comes at last the happy day
When she pulls level in the race
And sees at last her husband's face.

And maybe there will be the few
Years left to the married two
When she will go ahead and break
The gale's force for an old man's sake.

[187]

On the Green Carpet

The boy-children of Maine and the men seem somehow all of a part and piece out in an air that seems untainted by time. Young and old cease to be different. Here I prove it in that day which is the surest sign of Spring, the day of the painting of the farm's and family's boats:

Spring has come, though ice still hardens hollows,
Almost any day there will be swallows,
For father and the boys have shed their coats,
All hands are in the white-lead painting boats.

The cove is full of laughter and he-cries,
The small boy has two white and staring eyes
On the blind side of his breeches where he rested
On the plank where brushes have been tested.

Father has twin smooches on his chin,
He lays the good paint on, draws it out thin,
He caresses with wide arms and thighs
The curving wood, and love lights up his eyes.

The son upon the port side keeps the pace
With his father, sweeping the hard lace
Of lap-streaked pine, his round brush is alight
With lightning and the sharply-smelling white.

They have the baby where he can't upset
The paint-pail, he is underneath the net,
To his fellow men he waves and crows
Crisscrossed with meshes on his cheeks and nose.

Mother can keep her biscuits on the stove,
There is a love-affair down at the cove,

Green Maine

Women and food for once will have to wait,
Tonight the supper will be good and late.

Our Maine crops, measured as the world measures crops, are small and hard. Hard apples, small potatoes, and few to the hill. But because they grow over against the infinity and the endurance of the sea, our crops grow large and princely as poetry measures things. Small particulars prove the universals. Our wild roses are small, and fish-hooked with a hundred thorns to one bloom; yet roses were never so deeply colored and fierce in their beauty; they match themselves against the endless, ageless ocean. They are small outposts of eternal color and growth. These flowers, like the coast people, turn poems.

My Place Has Its Small Fruits

Too high under the Northern Lights to be
Fertile, too much the bare bones of the sea,
My place has its small fruits and hard flowers:
Crab-apples, brown men quiet as night hours,
The hardhack's lacy spires of purple flame,
Firs and waves no plows or boats can tame,
The high sweet cries of plovers, the gray ledges
With white eternal thunder for their edges,
Huckleberries tasting of sea and frost,
Dry everlasting-roses, lonely lost
Symphonies of bells rung by the waves,
Deer furrowing the ocean, the bright graves
Always looking to sea on the high hills,
Flute of thrush, the whisper of whippoorwills,
Fierce little boys as wiry as the deer
With freckles burning on them ear to ear,

On the Green Carpet

The pasture with crab-claws bleached whiter than snow,
Steep winding paths where men and women go
Forever single through the junipers.

Whatever lives in hard cones, thorns, or burrs
Against great wind and cold thrives here and shines:
Charity, the silver-running pines,
Independence, long-visored lobstermen,
The sharp high dory with the strength of ten
Other boats, the chickadees like sparks
Of fire on the snow, the rainbows' arcs
Picking out square houses like cut stones,
Light that gets inside the hollow bones,
The sound of song-sparrows coming through a gale
On islands far at sea, the coat of mail
Poor, common people wear through all their lives,
The ageless old men and the old young wives.

These are my flowers: the thorny pink wild briar
That scents the sea and sets cold rocks on fire,
Fringed gentians, sails above a harbor's steeple,
Marsh-rosemary, the quiet, hard, good people.

I have said how beautiful New England gravestones are as
they fit into the green carpet. On the blue-green carpet which
is the Maine coast this is especially so. It is the law of poetic
togetherness again. Life and death can go splendidly hand
in hand in the midst of such continuous splendor. Lichened
gravestones go well against walls of dark spruces, with stonewalls that keep the wild trees out. Here lie captains who
sailed all the seas and took these Welsh slates with them till
they should have use for them; here are captains' stones with
no captains below them, for the captains sleep in oceans on

he other side of the globe. Wild rabbits pause to wonder at
he death's-head cherubs in stone here; and Queen Anne's
ace imitates the lacework of weeping willows on ancient
slates. Small boys coming home from school pass their grandparents quiet on the hill; and somehow the small boys are
more careful of their schoolbooks, passing their grandparents
this way. Many farms have their own family lots, and old
men must lie happy here with small editions of them driv-
ing home the cows past the mounds where they lie. Such togetherness is a kind of immortality.

Even when the stonewalls have been cast down by the
frost and wild maples and hemlocks have come in at last into
the graveyard, it is the right thing to do to forgive the wild
things for coming back home. Deer eye these even white and
gray stones slanting all parallel in the sweet wild grass they
graze. The wild and tame are friends at last in a dusky green
truce. Man forgives the wild that won the battle of two centuries:

Foxes and Graves

When they came and told me there were foxes
In my great-grandfather's grave, then I was glad;
It is an old graveyard grown up with oak trees,
And nothing in a fox can make one sad.

I knew the graveyard once, but then I lost it;
Trees spring up quickly when young men are gone;
The oaks are sons of ones my forefather battled,
His own sons went away, but these stayed on.

There is nothing wrong about wild creatures coming
Back home again, if people move away,

On the Green Carpet

It is good to know small deer are walking
The floors where two-foot children did not stay.

And foxes are not creatures mean or common,
They are the needles of all forest kind,
So bright, so sharp, they get through all things growing;
I am sure my forefather would not mind.

Foxes take to graves when making burrows,
They like the soil that has been dug before;
A burrow is a grave, when you consider,
A lovely warm grave. And it has a door.

In death at last wounds are healed, the ancient cousinship is restored.

Sometimes a man, seeing these second and final burials in the oblivion of flaming maples of Autumn, seeing these family stones behind the kitchen which seem as natural as the gray stonewalls behind them, seeing men and women and children living so naturally with death, begins to have a strange feeling. It is as though all these tipped stones had nothing below them, as if the old dead had escaped the heavy mounds and sunken greensward after all and were still here in the men shining with sweat and the women planting sweetpeas. A man comes to believing that even death has never broken nor could ever break the continuity of man. Generations side by side; those on the waves, those under the waves, in the churchyard and in the barns, all going on together strong as ever; and the men of the future keeping step with them, pulling an oar behind them. Such is the sense of continuing indelible in an old place where man has lived hard for a long time and wakes and works, rests and sleeps, all in community. Time melts like a fog, and the steady strong sunlight seems forever and ever. The sea-captains and the fishermen are not a century apart but in the same boat rowing up the future which will never fade out of this amber and living now:

They Rowed, They Sang

They sang to the oars, their songs thinned in the firs,
They rowed, they sang, their voices climbed the sea,
Never was any coast a lace so fine,
Never a sea so like eternity!
Never an ocean so blue, so steep uphill;
They rowed, but they stayed forever still.

The rowers never knew how true they sang,
Terns snowed above them in an endless snow,
They were bronze, they were common lobstermen,
And they were bronze sea-captains long ago.
The white houses and the whitecaps gleamed as one,
The rowers were not all men but part sun.

Under the songs they sang the old bones whitened,
Their fathers rolled at peace under the reef,
Dark lobsters slid away from where they brightened,
The bones were proud, were long beyond belief;
On the beaches golden grandsons flew
Livelier than the plovers tipping the blue.

Songs and broad backs bending to long rhythm,
O such music ospreys wrote on sky!
O but the songs were sweet, the sun unending!
These men sang like men not meant to die;
They sang, they rowed past time up the high sea;
They sing loud now in blue eternity.

My father is here and now; my grandfather and his. The place they knew and loved and worked in is still theirs. They are a part of it. For I still know and love it and work in it. They are a part of me. There has been no shadow on this bright coast. The togetherness of Maine erases space and cancels out time; only man is important, not the names of particular men. So the lovely local, as always in poetry, rises and merges with the universal; these same seagulls snow always in the same sunshiny storm along all the azure coasts of the green and azure world.

Small, tired, local characters, bound for oblivion and a sure return to the green carpet that created them, suddenly take on themselves the wings of everlasting metaphor, the salvation of the enduring whole. They, being old and bound to die, in a sad time, are reborn, and they shine as one of the links of the chain never broken, wherein the same birds flow always over the land and sea, though the same birds remain never the same but are forever reborn and renewed. The sea gull becomes the phoenix.

Such was the case with Roxiney. She was an old unwanted woman. She had seen better days. A more tragic phrase than that is not to be found in Aeschylus or Sophocles. She lived in a bleak and windy Maine fishing village all by herself, all her friends being gone into the earth or into the distance. She had once been the center of all the mirth and liveliness of the little place, but now she lived in a run-down house away on the edge of things. She had had love, too often and in too many places, but love was over and gone now. The old ones gave her a wide berth, and the young ones thought of her as queer. She talked to herself, having no one else to talk to, no one else for company. She suffered not only from loneliness and neglect, but also from a deep sense of sin and a hard case of rheumatism. She was headed like an old schooner into a foggy doom. And then, out of her twin handicaps of rheumatism and a sense of sin, her chance came for metonymy, her chance to achieve the metaphor of belonging. She who had ceased to belong suddenly, in her agony, cried out her confession of belonging for good to the everlasting beauty of her place.

It was on a dark Fall day, when people in the fishing hamlet were bound over the bay for the revival meeting going on full cry over there. In the gray mist, as they were getting into their boats, someone spied Roxiney hanging pathetically about on the edge of things. "Why don't you come on over and get religion the way the rest of us are?" Someone said it as a joke. Roxiney did not take it so. She said she could not. Her rheumatism was bad again. She could not get into a dory with its high flaring sides. And, she added, she did not think it was right for her to go. She had not lived the kind of life that entitled her to salvation. She was sorry, but she couldn't go. She expressed her sorrow in metaphor. In her figure of speech she combined her hunger after religion with the wings of birds. Not the dove's. She did not know doves. They did not live in her windswept place. She combined her hunger with the wings of birds she knew, the coot and the loon. She said, "If I had the wings of a coot or a loon, I'd fly to Seal Harbor to my Jesus." She started a poem off. So I have finished it for her:

Roxiney Boody

When Fall winds began to blow,
There was Roxiney's tremolo:

"If I had the flippers of a seal,
I'd swim to Jesus, and he would heal."

When clams came frozen from their bed,
Repentance raised her cow-licked head.

"If I had the wings of a coot or a loon,
I'd fly to my Jesus in Malagoon!"

But Jesus and his lonesome eyes
Were ten miles as the seagull flies.

It was ten miles to Malagoon,
Ten watery miles under the moon.

And Roxiney Boody's knees
Were gnarled with old age and disease.

"If I had a dory of seasoned pine,
Jesus would straighten these knees of mine!"

But Jesus and the Reverend Smith were there
And sinners washed out white and fair.

And old Roxiney spent her groans
Along Sabino's icy stones.

"If I could fly with the ring-necked geese,
I'd go to my Savior and make my peace."

But Roxiney's sins were great,
They weighed her down with a millstone's weight.

The far-off days of a dancing spree
When Roxy danced *Hull's Victory,*

And every fisherman, stout or thin,
Swore she was the lightest one to spin!

Light as the down of the high bull-thistle,
Foot of the deer, and a plover's whistle!

Long-ago nights of velvet stars
When she was kissed under dewy spars.

Nights of loving among the nets
And shoes drenched with May violets.

Laughter and tripping under the dawn,
And the sun came up, and youth had gone.

"If I was a shad with a silver side,
I'd swim to Jesus and be his bride!

"And my young skin would be like silk,
Jesus would wash me white as milk!"

The Fall winds blew and blent their woe
With old Roxiney's tremolo.

This was a woman made clean and redeemed by the clean
birds of the sea. The least stone, rejected by the builders, can
become the cornerstone of the whole fabric. So Roxiney.
So many another small human being in the wide meadows

where sea and green fields join in the brotherhood, out o
time and out of space, of the clean and the enduring. So th
winds, and the airy children of the winds, saved a lost one a
last. Roxiney, like numberless outdoors others, found salva
tion in the outdoors in a song.

Such a redeemer is green Maine.

VI

CATHEDRALS OF THE NORTH

6. Cathedrals of the North

In the pages that follow, I am going to close into a smaller area than ever, and I propose to celebrate a single feature on the green carpet that is New England, that is Maine.

Nations can be summed up by symbols. The axe in the rods for Rome. The columned façade that is reason and the Greeks. The ear of Indian corn—lovelier in its stylized husks and silk than the stylized acanthus, so like the monoliths of New York and Chicago with lighted windows for their kernels at night—there is North America and home. Or a freckled barefoot boy in overalls, with a hound-dog. It is possible to get a nation down in a few lines of life, to put the spirit of a culture into one of its fabrications.

If I had to choose a building to stand for America, it would not be one of those tall silver monoliths of New York City, though. I would go to the country, to the green carpet, for my symbol. It would be barns. The barn is America at its fragrant and warmest best. It stands for the genius of a nation built of rich soil and fat cattle.

The vast Pennsylvania-Dutch barns of Pennsylvania, Maryland, and Virginia, with archaeology, ethnology, folk-lore, and morality built into their distinctive brick-work, raftering, and stone, are typical and thoroughly American buildings. They have Old World German charms and "hex" marks built into their wood and stone to fend off evil from New

World corn and cattle, but they smell of the western world. I know of one Pennsylvania farmer who had eight daughters and wanted a son. But his ninth child turned out another girl. He had a barn building, near Chambersburg. So he up and put all nine girls into his gable, in wide petticoats, to preside over his wheat.

Yet as a New Englander, I do not think of those great Pennsylvania-Dutch barns as barns. They do not take the cows and horses in, except under their overhangs for tea. Then they turn them out into the weather again. It never could happen in my part of the world. There we have to take our cows, our horses, our hens, and our sheep, right into our houses, the weather being what it is for six months of the twelve, right into the family, right into our hearts! Perhaps we have loved our little Morgan colts and our stiff-legged calves more than other people have theirs because we have had fewer of them and have had to take them into the family so much. I think of the immense red barns of Vermont, the great gray barns of New Hampshire, colored with storm and time, the white vast barns of Maine. These barns dwarf our houses. They are as fine in their architecture, in their mouldings and finish, as our houses; they often have the same green blinds at their windows exactly as our parlors do; they are clapboarded; and they have cupolas on top, to lift up the mind at the same time as they ventilate the hay, like Chinese temples. Indeed, many of those cupolas did, in idea, come from China in the days when our farmers were also merchant princes and traded at the four corners of the globe.

These barns are our northern American glory. Larger than some of the châteaux along the Loire, larger than many

European cathedrals, they are our religion. They are our cathedrals. For warm worship and daily rituals of fealty to life have gone on in them, time out of mind, for centuries. If the old Gothic cathedrals hark back to the German forests with the sun slanting through high tree trunks, making a solemn religious light, our barns are even closer to nature; for they are built high enough to take in the sky and half out-of-doors. Blue swallows swoop through the upper inter-planetary spaces above the mows; nations of birds and beasts congregate and live here. Such vast temples of harvest are capable of taking in all the green year. The green carpet of our North, so brief, so perishable, can be rolled up and saved here, from the gales, from the snows, from the long ruin of our Winter. Even our field mice come in from the fields to this Summer we have saved and housed in sweet hay. The cattle come in, the suns of pumpkins are rolled in, our bean-fields are stacked in the golden glooms; all Summer is housed in mows that smell of honey of the red clover and the white. We house all nature home. We make these buildings universes that save all life when all life outside dies bitterly away, and nothing warm or alive is left between the cold side of the earth and the nearest stars. Here we make our stand against inertia, and take the green world in, to save it for another harvest.

Winter Sparks

Cold Winter evening rounds the white world over
With arch of stars so far they are like frost,
The few small farmhouses have shrunk and drifted
Far apart, and their small lights are lost

On the Green Carpet

In this night made luminous with snow,
The ways between the farms are long to go,
Only the little foxes here have crossed.

Yet in these shrunken farms and these far houses
Go little lamps and lanterns one by one,
And the eyes of eager cows and horses
Are kindled by these cousins of the sun.
Heat and life are here still in the only
Warm lights between the cold earth and the lonely
Stars so far away their heat is done.

Life is here though dwindled to a dozen
Steps between the grain-bin and the hay,
Love is here in numbed but tender gestures
Though love has but little now to say.
In the scattered sparks of this sad night
Are sleeping the high bonfires, the delight
Which will blow up and be a Summer's day.

The farmer must take over the Creator himself in the days of
the yearly death in nature, in the nights of our ice and snow.

Going out to this cathedral of our green religion, of our
rural welfare, at night under the stars is a starry business.
When a man goes out to feed his stock by starlight, the lantern in the man's hand pushes his shadow off the earth, and
his shadow out there among the stars, in the graveyard of
time, makes the stars come out all the brighter and loom
larger. For once a man carries the sun in his hand, and he
sees what effect the bulk of his body has on the stars. He is
bound then to feel he is something vast. And when he gets
to his barn and feels the worship in the eyes of the beasts he
feeds, he is bound to feel he has deity in him.

Sitting here now in his barn at the milking, in the cold of the night, the farmer cannot help feeling his great importance to the world of the living, as he acts the warm warden of what is left that has heat in it. Milking a cow is as fine a poem as man has ever had his hands on. But milking a cow in the Winter is a lovelier poem than milking a cow in the Summer. For when a man milks in the Winter, it is always dark on the world, his lantern and the stars in his cows' eyes are the only lights on the world's side between him and the first stars. When a man milks in the Winter, it is always cold, and he and the cow are the only warm things on the cold face of the earth. When a man milks in the Winter, he and his stock are all that are left alive to compete with inertia. And he sits there competing with the inertia of space in a dead or sleeping world, fights his single fight, and comes off victorious. A man then cannot but feel that he is a solemn and special part of the universe. He cannot but know the poem he takes part in for the poem it is:

Winter Milking

Five o'clock, and snow knee-deep,
More in the air before men sleep.
The night is thick a foot behind,
A foot before, I stumble blind
With too much light in one small space,
I lower the lantern from my face.
Now I am in, and shut the door,
Stamp the snow off on the floor,
Set the lantern by the sill.
The tie-up suddenly grows so still
I hear a squeaky mouse in the bin,

Vast, sweet breaths are taken in
Behind the door. I dole out grain,
And now the breaths rush out again,
Stanchions rattle, bodies stir;
I open the door on minever,
Velvet, sunshine in sleek hair,
And honey and clover in the air.
Round eyes beam on me, tongues caress
Blue nostrils wide with eagerness.
I put the feed-boxes in place,
Hunger furnishes the grace.

I take my stool and pail and sit
Under a cow and stroke each teat
With fingers in sequence down the five,
I feel her milk come down alive,
Tinkling stream, then thick and thicker,
Between my knees ascends the liquor
Until the warmth of it goes deep
Into my thigh bones as I keep
The pail in place. I lean my head
Against her flank above me spread.
I feel my blood and hers as one,
Full of contentment and of sun.
Over the ridgepole whirls new snow,
And I bow my head and know
That for this moment we are kin,
This creature I have taken in
And I whose kind rose so above
The roots of earth we missed such love
As I feel now upon my brow
Pressed to the velvet of a cow.
Under the thousand miles of night
I sit in a tiny world of light,

And shapes of unknown woe and death
Go over me in the sobbing breath
Of the storm outside, but I sit calm
With love on my forehead like a palm.

These wooden worlds into which we roll our green country carpet at the fall of the leaf and the blossoming of the first frost are, in my part of the North, joined right on to our houses by easy stages of ell and woodshed and carriage-house. They are all of a piece with our living-rooms, all under one roof. We probably have had to evolve this marriage of house and barn because of our deep snows. That is the economy of the matter. Yet not the poetry. For I like to think, knowing the New England character as I do, that this reticent human being, this mute Milton, would have worked out this joining of the barn and house even though there had been no snow at all outdoors. He wanted to have his barn close to him, for here at last he has the chance to let the emotions he feels he must suppress in the parlor have full rein. Love is at home in the barn, and the demonstration of affection. The man lavishes on new lambs and baby calves the endearments the New England code of family living requires him to be sparing of when he is with his children in the house. With his barn children it is no such thing. So I know we would have connected our barns to our houses even if our climate had been that of Florida! This occidental parlor has always been the leading New England living-room. It *is* an occidental parlor, for all the best farmsteads of ours are oriented, as carefully as old churches are, as carefully as our beds are; and our front doors and our parlors face the east. But our front parlors were used most sparingly in the past, chiefly for courtships and funerals, not the routines of living.

I remember my own farm parlor. It was a room dedicated more to the dead than the living. Wreaths of dead uncles' hair hung there. One lock of my grandfather's hair tied his bow to his bass-viol. The family *Bible,* with its birth dates and death dates, was there. It was a room unheated in Winter; one courted rheumatism being there. The sofas and chairs were horsehair and severe on a small boy's seat. The forbidden books were there: the unexpurgated *Arabian Nights,* the *Family Doctor.* I had to explore its Anatomical Man under the sofa, and when an aunt entered suddenly, I had to shut the book up quickly, often with parts of the Anatomical Man not decently back in his body but unfolded all over the floor. It was a place, that parlor, for holding the breath. A rare room, and not for everyday use.

But our barns in New England have been our real living-rooms. Here the warmest part of our farm living has always been done. These barn rooms, the tie-up, the horse-stall, cow-stall, and henhouse, have had more living going on continuously in them, likely, than any other buildings in North America. More living by the night as well as the day; more by the year as well as the nights and days; more living for a lifetime as well as a sum of years; and, when one considers what loyalties and affections have warmed these rooms more than all the lanterns that have shone here, more living for the after-lifetime, for eternity, than for merely the stretch of any man's life.

Such rooms, if any rooms can be called that, are holy

rooms. Here the farmer has acted the doctor and stood off death. Here he has been the midwife and ushered in legions of little calves and horses into the light. Here, late at night, in times of trouble and worry, when a man mostly grows into his manhood, he has worked after hours, a twenty-four-hour day, sweat fierce sweat and fought and lost and won many a fight. Here in unremembered evenings of utter peace, in a blessed quiet, he has bedded down his cows, stroked the lambs' cloth-like symmetries, heard the low whispers of peace in the easy cuds of his cows, stood in the midst of such loyalty and trust as is hard to come on among men, or in cities. Here he has been warmed by the suns of his cattle's sunflower eyes. He has stood close to kingliness in a bull, to queenhood in cows. Hera, Queen of heaven, borrowed her eyes from the ox. He has stood in the midst of contentment and worship in his barn, and grown better for it. A bad man could no more be a good farmer than an angler for trout be a contentious and quarrelsome man. I think there is no other place on earth like a Winter barn or a Summer barn at night to teach a man tenderness and mildness and charity.

In this house of the harvests of the North, the farmer stands as the center, as the director of the miracles of repeated birth, and growth and decay. Here he sees life begin on wobbly calves getting for the first time to their feet but knowing, by the looks of the way they go at it, from eternity just where milk is to be had. Here he sees eggs beat like hearts, and golden chicks peck their way to the air. He has seen death come gently here and like an old friend to a horse that has been like a part of himself through many years, and has shed bitter tears unashamed which custom

[211]

has kept him from shedding at his brother's deathbed. If feeling one's way into friendship with all forms of life be a chief business of man, as it surely is the main duty of the poet, then the keeper of the northern barn has opportunities for his psychic and spiritual enlargement it is given to no other wardens to know. Lonely nights and lonely vigils here, but nights walled around by trust and belief. If anyone doubts there is such a thing as good will in the world, he needs only to go to the nearest barn to see it in flower.

The barn is a good neighborhood of the four-footed, the two-footed, and the feathered and winged. It is community. One warm little universe under the reaches of unwilling, uncomprehending, unfeeling night, one city of refuge in the warfare of the world, a man-made, man-warmed world emerging under the cold January starlight. Friendliness in an oasis in the vast deserts of space.

Think of the best a man can want of life. Tact, friendliness, courtesy, decorum, good neighborliness. And all these can be found shining in the warmest of our temples, the barn. A great stallion is gentle naturally to the farmer's small child; a vast bull is careful not to hurt a small girl. Young animals are born with great courtesy on them. I recall a Summer evening in a barnyard:

The Gracious and the Gentle Thing

The three young heifers were at Summer supper
In the cowpen munching new-mown hay,
Their eyes suffused with sweetness of red clover,
It was no time to pass the time of day.
Their chins went side to side, their cheeks were bulging
Indecorously, and they were eating more;

Cathedrals of the North

I was a stranger, I had no introduction,
They had never laid eyes on me before.

Yet when I patted each young lady's sleekness,
Each young lady's lips grew bland and still,
She left the hay that sweetened the whole evening
And beamed on me with eyes deep with good will.
She kissed my hand where it lay on the fence-rail
And breathed her sweetness in my smiling face;
She left her supper, turned her slender beauty
Instantly to practice of good grace.

I stood there below the azure evening
With miles of tender thrushes all around
And thought how up and down the land I never
So natural a courtesy had found
As this night in a barnyard with three heifers.
The gracious and the gentle thing to do,
With never any lesson in good manners,
These innocent and courteous creatures knew.

Cows take a kindly interest in the pullets. Cats and cows consort. A cow in Winter is a gracious stove to all the barn cats. I have seen four at a time warming themselves along a cow's back. And the cats are careful to keep their claws sheathed. Cats, predatory and unfriendly in the open, or even in a house, learn gentleness and friendliness in a Winter barn. If peace be anywhere, it is in such a place.

Formula for Peace

The happiest beings on this earth,
Though not in heaven, live close by it;
This is their formula for peace:
Mice and milk and warmth and quiet.

[213]

On the Green Carpet

Cats that live in great farm barns
Enjoy a universe apart;
Security is its high hay walls,
Silence is its dusky heart.

It never rains, it never snows,
Summer is forever there,
Clover, grass immortalized
Sweeten forever the still air.

The cats unruffled in their fur
Hear winds outside shaking the world;
They do not have to hunt, their prey
Comes to them where they lie upcurled.

Mice fattened on a bygone June,
Mice fragrant of a spicy May
Come through the January frost
To serve these cats lapped warm in hay.

When zero weather bites the earth,
Cats go to the tie-up, and they lie
Along the backs of sleepy cows,
They drowse in peace upon July.

Morning and evening there is milk
Warm from udders for their diet:
The world runs like an endless song—
Mice and milk, sweet heat, sweet quiet.

Cows take a kindly view of young colts; mares act with understanding and charity towards boisterous bull-calves. Animals make allowances. Animals in barns are on their best behavior. It is almost as if they knew they must stand together against the evil of hard weather, against hunger and long nights. They are quiet and patient even when hungry. They eat their supper decorously, and their manners are naturally good. This community in barns is an ancient one. It has learned through thousands of Winters. It remembers. It proves the beautiful existence of a memory much longer than any individual being, of an incorporated and continuing good will. It is the culmination of a long league of living things standing together against inertia.

Here under one roof, the old poems of the pastoral convention, of the ancient bucolics, make still a warm presence in a cold mechanical world. The history of mankind's own federation for peace, against the common enemy of hunger and desolation and death is repeated here every day, every night in Winter. Here is poem on poem, old as the hills, young as tonight's new-born calf. Under cover here, the green poem of the green world flourishes, without the sun or the wind or the blue sky, with all the earth gone gray or brown or deathly white and still.

No man can ever exhaust the poems a barn is. I have tried in my time, but I have made but a beginning. Three new poems spring up each time I track one to its source. I have been called a barn poet. I am proud to be called so. That is not always meant, let me tell you, as a compliment. It is a way some metropolitan critics have of annihilating a poet. They think that barns are rather naïve, archaic places, elementary, that my poetry of barns is, therefore, childish, jejune, old-fashioned, traditional, banal, superficial, naïve. If patience and a tough will to live, if courage and endurance, if charity, if honor and brotherhood, neighborhood, a sense of the dignity and rightness and beauty of the sex act and relationships are banal, naïve, and childish, God knows we have come too long a distance from the barn, and we ought to go back to it as soon as we can and learn there some good health to counteract the poison of Freudianism, some depth to save us from our superficial sophistications, some good will to make an end of our growing distrust in our urbanized world.

I hold that barns are one of the best proofs of my thesis in these chapters. That man looks and behaves his handsomest in the country, in a green world. Man fits himself best for life when he fits into nature and becomes a part of storm and fine weather, of the tides and moons, as fishermen do; the nature of silence and repose of tall and quiet trees, of white water and dark water, as good hunters and fishermen do; of the loam and the mold, with grass and cattle, as best farmers do. Before he can establish himself with his fellows, a man must learn his ABC's from his mother, the lady in green. A man looks his best in the green symphony that created him. And when a man, a northern man, has to take green nature's part, take her indoors and keep Summer herself green, in a barn, in the long dead white days, in the long, savage white nights of hungry stars, then a man has the chance to become, himself, a universal power, even though small, a creator, in handling himself the miracles of birth and death, breeding and increase. This plain man, this common farmer, has endless chances to see the circles of life, to enter those circles, to see the whole circle as a whole. To see there is no beginning, no end, no large, no small, but only rightness and rhythm. This common man has an opportunity the philosopher or the man of religion must envy his having. This farmer handles homely matter: muck, dirt, manure, lust, sweat, the deadly repetitions of hard labor; yet he has the chance to see how these, too, have a glory on them as necessary parts to the whole, how these are, in the whole view, as lovely as angels and cherubim, how all are parts in a whole starry business.

In the concentrated and contracted and consecrated country taken into a man's home in his Winter barn, man learns, as in other businesses, that he is related to a vast whole. His business is the business of getting on good terms with the vast. If he is a good farmer, he does all this naturally, without the necessity of putting it into words. The words are but one aspect of it. Most farmers I know haven't the words to express this vast poem, this act, in; but most farmers I know, without the words, know their handsome way about in it. That is why I have found so many poems in them, in their barns. I could never have written the poems unless they had acted them, been them. I am merely speaking for many silent comely men.

Maybe the fact I came up to maturity on a farm has much to do with it. I know a good many of my barn poems from having been in them, even as a small farmer in knee trousers, from having acted in their warm midst. Now, having the words and knowing other men who have remained and grown up and grown old on farms, I can speak better, out of a double experience and a doubled sympathy.

I know other poets, other writers, even in this urbanized time, feel as I do about the country. There is Elizabeth Coatsworth, the poet, Gladys Hasty Carroll, the novelist.

They will bear me out in my thesis that the green carpet is the handsomest place to see the dance of life. There is Henry Beston, another good neighbor of mine, of all men in these red and black years, one having the wisest and greenest of minds. With both French and English civilizations in him, he, even more than Thoreau, sees in the green fields and the equity and equilibriums of the seasons the best sculptors of manners, the best artisans of goodness in man. For courtesy and nobility he goes, not to the ballrooms or the cities, but to the woods of the lower St. Lawrence, to the hard, small farms of Nobleboro, Maine. A natural poet, he writes his best prose from the midst of the good green life.

The poems of the North housed in barns are like the stars of an August night. There is no end to their brightness, to their exquisite sequence and consequence. These poems are like the webbings of a fine feather. They fit each into each. One grows from another.

Where shall one begin in such labyrinths of loveliness? It is best to burst in at random. The mere process of the seasons in the barn rituals offers poems enough. For barns have their seasonal characteristics. The Summer barn is a different universe from the Winter barn. It is a hot and dark universe. The light cuts into its massy glooms with thin and solid golden knives through every crack. Hot night holds the upper space. A beetle hangs in the middle air and shines like a whirling diamond. Swallows dart like blue bullets through the open doors. The barn is like an oven and smells so. But on the other side of the year, the Winter barn is full of supernal light; the frosted windows filter light even to the topmost beams; the tangled nets of Summer's spiders show up sharp and clear. Every nailhead is a cushion of frost. The mows smell more like Summer than Summer itself. The rustle of mice goes on as they eat away their very house. The Fall barn is a great silence and only a narrow aisle of light between full mows. The Spring barn is a restless, empty, forgotten world. The cows yearn at their stanchions for the green that is beginning to prick through the earth outside; the mows are chaff. But the heart of the place may shine some years with this year's new boat, with men and boys and sweet-smelling white pine. The doors, come May, may open wide, not for hay, but for the coming forth of this white-pine new daughter of the farm, and the boat slide into the sea. For my barns look out to sea.

Haying time at the barn is Homer time. Under white thunderheads the days of July are sagas, and the barn is center of all existence. The thunder of loads shakes the barn, the loads go in, the horses dig in their front hooves as they slant up the runway, the small boys lie face down to keep from being brushed off their moving mountain, the horses roar through the barn, and their wide-eyed heads emerge at the smaller door on the barn's other side. Then the master-pitcher stands on the rack, sweats and subsides as he unloads in ten vast forkfuls, and brown boys must look alive as they tread the mows and stow away, or they will be lost till next May! The horses have their nostrils outside in the open air, but their frothed bodies are in the sweet heat between the haymows. Men stand and glow all bare Red Indians to their waists, glossed with sweat. Never such sweetness poured out on the world as that the well-made hay pours out over the world from the big double barn-doors in haying time. Now muscles swell, and tempers flash like the lightning forking the west; stories are short, appetites vast and wide; small boys are at full cry with Indian legs and pockets stuffed with blind field-mice, heads full of red clover and breeches full of Satan; and lusty life stands at tip-top highwater mark.

I do not know of a lovelier poem in the world than the poem of the last load of hay. I saw this poem over and over as a boy. I knew it then for a poem though I knew nothing then about poetry. As the last groaning hayrack came in, it carried, between the standing driver's tired hot feet, a cluster of wild briar-roses. The deep-pink, gold-centered flowers, that will never be brought into the house but wilt and drop their heart-shaped petals at once inside, that wither in ten minutes' time. But there they were crowning the last load. There those roses always were on every last load of the Summer. They were a ritual. Nobody ever explained the ritual to me. Nobody had any need to. It was right to have those roses there. Roses were the good last touch to haying. I always drew in my breath with delight when I saw them appear, and it wasn't merely that they meant the end of a lot of righteous hard work, of raking and windrowing. I know now, as a man, the exquisite why of the whole thing. Behind that lovely extra touch, the roses, there was hard New England common sense. The hay should all be in before the brief wild Summer rose fell. Hay harvested after those flowers were gone and there were none of them to ride the rack, was half-hearted hay, the juices that should have been in it would be ebbed all back into the ground. The hay would be like the swarm of bees in July—"not worth a fly." The thing was one more comely moral from the calendar. That spray of wild roses was an insurance on good hay. Those roses were hard logic. Yet it all goes to show how the finest poetry is rooted in logic, in bronze and iron consequence. Wild roses fall as the calendar of good hay runs out. It is in the flood and ebb of the seasons, out among the tides of the sea and the march of stars such logic and poetry grow, one and indivisible forever.

Last Load

July leaned his white and thundery head
High over the high last hayrack going in,
The wheels, the horses' tails were lost in sweet,
On the edge of the world was the low thundering;
The boys were flattened pants on a moving world,
The farmer stood wet bronze in clinging clothes;
This was the year's last load, and on the gold
Between his feet lay the branch of pink wild rose.

Great-grandfather's father put the rose there first,
The blossoms had crowned each last load since his day;
There was no reasoning a habit like this one out,
Like youths making love like men, things were this way;
Though wits, if wits worked hard, could work it out:
Hay to be housed its thrifty sweetest must
Be in before the last wild briar-rose
Had shed and was a cup of golden dust.

It might be this would be the last rose there
And this the last load of last loads for good;
The farmer was deep Winter on his hair,
The farm was being crowded by wild wood,
Boys were looking townwards, and machines
Were pushing horses and hand-farming so

A year might see kingdoms of sentiment
Crumble like all kingdoms of long ago.

There is another as handsome poem of hay. It was set
down in bare arabic numerals on the main beam of the barn.
A mere succession of numbers. Yet behind those numbers
was the whole history of the rise and fall of that farm which
had this barn for heart. It was the annual total of loads of
hay brought in. The log of a family's prosperity and pride.
You could follow the years through there, the lean years of
drought, the fat years of rain, in a poem of peace, a catalogue
of high ships of green peace surpassing the catalogue of ships
in Homer. Believe it, men's lives, the lives of their small sons
and daughters, as well as their little calves, depended upon
those figures on that beam. A rise in the figures meant new
babies. As the sons grew and left the farm and Winter settled
on the farmer's hair, the figures fell off. And where the figures cease, a poem of warm life ends.

Hay-Log

Out here in this old barn is family history
More telling than boughs upon a family-tree
Which tell what lusty man begat which offspring;
This is a century of sweet certainty.
These figures on the beam tot up the total
Of loads of hay hauled in each sweet July;
In these no good, no bad years could be hidden
Any more than rings of years in trees could lie.

Words can deceive, and pride may cover trouble;
But here is a ledger of the truthful years,
A log of russet timothy, red clover,

Of slender heifers and the wide-faced steers;
These chronicles tell what years had the iron,
What years had the silver spoons in the mouth,
Here are the years of good rains and the whistling,
Here the years of heartaches and the drouth.

Where this figure swells upon the timber
The farmer's circle widened by a son,
Here where the Summer's figures start to dwindle
The farm's boys started leaving one by one;
These shrinking numbers sadly tell the story
Of debts and trees closing in on every side,
This blank space is as solemn as a tombstone,
Here the figures cease, the family died.

Other poems there are in this sequent symphony of barn
living. There is the ritual of the cows coming in from pasture
at night, plump and drowsy with feeding, with the white-
ankled small boy bringing up the rear, and the stars coming
out as the cows come in. Slow deep poetry of a square bronze
bell under a cow's chin. The cows' eyes big in the Summer
dusk. The sibilant peace of the streams of Summer milk in
the tin pail's foam. The dim orchestras of swarming gnats,
the sweet whispers of cuds of fragrant clover. There is the
poem of pitching down the hay in the months when the
pasture is dead or dying, the straining stanchions, the curling
rough tongues, the sweet breaths, the perfume of last Summer's grass and daisies falling like a benison from the darkness on high, the rayed beams of the farmer's lantern and the
aureoles common light makes of hay chaff and dust. There
is that other poem of bedding down the stock for night.
There is that jubilant Spring poem of letting the cows out

to the first blades of grass. Here is the coarser poem of cleaning out the cowstalls, the heady reek of what will be bean-blossoms and tall silken corn, come Summer.

There is that last ritual of the barn's night when the farmer goes his quiet rounds, seeing that all is fast and safe, all comfortable and peaceful for the night. It is the peak of the farmer's long day. He stands with his lantern between mows, hears the rhythm of cuds beyond him in the tie-up, the stir of relaxed bodies. His lantern, it is very likely, shows his breath about him—for the cold months outnumber the warm in this wooden universe he presides over. The stars shine in at the high panes. The man stands weary but responsible on his peak of peace. If there are any five other moments in a man's year to compare with these, I do not know them.

These North American cathedrals have poems for their history, of course. No one man made them. No one man however broad of back or good with the axe was equal to their magnitude and magnificence. They began as communal structures, just as their Gothic cousins in stone and glass and timber began, the mediaeval cathedrals of England and France. Whole communities turned out to hew their timbers and shape them on the flat; whole communities of neighbors gathered for their raising. The men lifted their four walls with ropes and sweat, clamped them together with iron, clapped on the roof. A mountain of white pine stood up from nothing in one day. And the men's wives served a vast supper in the shadow of the new cathedral for hay.

Of course, there are lighter poems in barns. The barn cats supply a lighter touch. The gathering of the gray clan and the mewing at milking-time; the warming of Winter toes

on the ridgepoles of the patient cows. The sleek total content
of a cat's sleeping out a blizzard on a cow is a good poem.
Then there are always the hens. The henhouse is a house of
comedy. Both Plautus and Aristophanes keep alive among
the feathered members of the green carpet family.

Hens in Winter

Winter is a far more fit
Time for hens than most admit.
They are not their best outside,
The world of trees is much too wide
For their essential comeliness.
One so easily can miss
Their artificial, tailored grace
Out where weathered swallows race.
There is in a hen's neat turban
Something planned and very urban.
Rains and winds and noble weathers
Rough her temperament and feathers.
And hens depend on company,
Gossip and garrulity,
To achieve completest sense
Of being central and immense.

So a henhouse banked with snow
Is the nearest place to go
To see the virtues of a crowd,
To hear life have her say aloud.
And nothing's nearer the comic sock
Than a hen that tries to walk
Through the wild and frigid white
Blossoms of a Winter's night.
The only wild part is the track
She prints on snow in coming back.

[225]

The henhouse has rituals deep in color and life. The feeding of the hens, the chaos and total disintegration when the farmer's wife brings in her pan of hot corns. The squawking and jostling. Then, as crops fill and hens grow one-sided, the gradual restoration of caste distinctions and decorum. The snubbings and the nasty nice manners. The restoration of amorousness. The rooster scratches up a large kernel, drops it and drops it from his beak and attracts his favorite hen, she comes running, and invariably chanticleer gobbles the kernel up himself, and treads her very gravely and handsomely. She never learns the subterfuge. Or does she, and keeps quiet about it for the sake of love? As Pertelote never learned to do.

Here are poems of burnished comb—"batailed, as it were a castel-wal," of crimson hackles, bronze feathers, bodies clothed in snow and fire, or in tortoise and flame. Poems of personality and promenading. The small boy cracking up crabs for the hens, and the rooster's keeping his distance and warning his harem against this incipient male. No hilarity of Plautus can match a hen, just become a mother on the nest, screaming the house of hens into a bedlam over her achievement. There is the poem of going to roost; the pathos of a chickless hen trying to steal the downy charges from a busy nurse. There is the furor of brooding, and the pure comedy of breaking up a setting-hen, she standing in water and still persisting in the instincts of motherhood though it damps her feathers and soul to brood the cold stuff. There are the poems of the hiding away of nests in the haymow, and the hunting for eggs in dim, fragrant corners of the universe; the poem of gathering in the white and brunette eggs hot from the nests, so pleasing to the palms on a Winter day. These feathered rituals have no end.

I remember a Winter barn poem like something sixteenth-century-Flemish and breathless. The high barn-doors were open a crack, and the low January sun sparkled with frost came in and spread a carpet of pure gold between the deep umber mows. Three standing pitchforks leaned long shadows the barn's length, the shadows bent right-angles, and went up the mow. A cat curled into utter content with the sun's warmth, with paws folded in under her, sopped up the brief Summer of this setting January sun.

There is that tall fountain-poem of the barn elm. Higher than the highest barn, massive in its trunk, it stands an airy forest and drips shadow and lacework of leaves and twigs over the white clapboards and gables of the noonday Summer barn, fairy lace and enchantment over the white clapboards under the full March moon. This tree is always there by the barn, like the yew in the English churchyard, the tallest of New England elms. Lovely poem often a century old. It is the largest elm of all because its roots are in the fertility of the seepage of a hundred years of cow and sheep droppings. It is not a tree; it is cows and horses and sheep turned into a green mountain of leaves and loveliness. And it is also the lightning-rod and savior of the barn it covers. It takes the lightning on one of its score of boughs, pours it into the earth, and saves the barn from the death by flame. Once again beauty is rooted in utility, and once more New England logic grows and flows from a poem's shape. The bronze chain of interdependence has no beginning and no end. The togetherness which is reason and poetry has no end.

[227]

But the end of these cathedrals of communities of men and beasts, as the end of all great and lovely things, Rheims Cathedral and the Parthenon, as the end of all tall men, is elegy. For these cathedrals are pine, and pine decays. These cathedrals are tall, and tall things attract the lightning, as the kings in Greece did, Agamemnon, Oedipus. These are doomed things. Sooner or later, by the quick death of lightning or the slow "smokeless burning of decay," these buildings will go into the ground. And something peculiarly and sweetly American, when they go, will go into the earth with them.

The Doomed

Doom hangs over these high white cathedrals
Of cows and colts, short Summers saved in hay;
Little bronze boys, the tanned tall men who kept them
Full of life and whistling did not stay.
Each year the Northern Lights of Fall find fewer
Barns standing white and brave against decay.

Sooner or later, the barns of old New England
Like Oedipus and Agamemnon must
Attract the ire of lightning or the whirlwind
And bow their wooden beauty to the dust;
They will sink in gales or stand in fire,
And on their bleached bones rot will work its lust.

Heavy snows, light worms, man-fire or lightning
Take these temples of labor one by one;
You come upon their graves in spreading thickets,
Carts with high wheels which never again will run,
Planks which hold up nothing but slight rabbits,
A sleigh on its runners under the August sun.

Cathedrals of the North

Quick flame by night or slow flame of decay—
These roofs raised by the hands of a neighborhood,
Empty now of men and sweet-breathed cattle,
Will return to the wild as rotten wood.
And when the last of these barns go, a history
And a republic will be gone for good.

But even sadder is when these great houses, dedicated to
warm, crowding life, stand empty on our horizons and hills,
with no life in them. New England is full of these sad poems
that are deserted barns. They are sadder even than the thousands of miles of stonewalls, which are the sweat and labor
and fealty to life of thousands of sturdy men and little boys,
running over hills, lost in the deep woods, wasted, keeping
nothing out and keeping nothing in. For stonewalls can
exist in a kind of tough completeness by themselves; but
barns have no existence beyond the warm creatures they
housed. Empty, they are deep sorrow.

Deserted Barns

Deserted barns are sadder even than houses;
For when an old house goes down to decay,
For all the empty cupboards, empty sashes,
You feel the people have only gone away,
And they are keeping house in other places,
They have the light of life still on their faces,
And they might come back home here some fine day.

But when a barn runs down and blue sky shows
Through the roof where bright-eyed heifers stood
And mows hold only cobwebs to the rafters,
You feel, somehow, that life is gone for good;

There never will be any resurrection
For these bones, the cows' child-like affection
You could not ever restore here if you would.

Houses have more to them than the people,
They have a personality in pine,
A dignity in wall-papers and their stair-rails;
With no one there, they still can breathe and shine.
But barns have nothing but their hay and horses,
When these are gone, and only the swallow crosses
Their silences, death takes them as his shrine.

The cry of baby lambs forever is muted,
Gone for good and all the rooster's crow,
High rooms to hold all Summertime will welcome
No tenants now but ruinous frost and snow.
These houses huge for happiness and clover
Need colts and new-born calves to tide them over,
And when these go, the souls of sweet barns go.

These lost cathedrals stand for a new economy, an economy that leaves men and cattle out as entities in themselves, an economy of the factory technique that has drained the poetry out of our modern farms. New barns rise and shine, in steel and glass, but they are factories. The men working in them are day-laborers, night-laborers, not farmers. These barns are factories of specialized farming, with machines to milk the cows, machinery to do the unloading and stowing of the hay. The factorization of the world goes on; the old farmers by hand and heart go out of the world, and the green poems they created go with them. Machines clear our forests, plant our wheat, reap, and almost eat it and us up. Farms are urbanized and regimented. Our milk is sterilized and pasteurized out of the warm miracle a small boy used to dip his nose into, before the milk-pail went to the house, into a mere matter of vitamins and calories. Life and poetry are sterilized out of the earth.

The older barns, made of a pine too precious now to be used in houses, stand on our hills as mournful reminders of the poetry we have lost out of life. The age that raised them and kept them warm and full seems already something out of Homer. Something out of a saga. Too expensive to be kept up, they settle into the soil that raised them. The large farm families, the dozen boys who kept them alive have gone with the pioneers out among the stars. The hierarchy of Anglo-Saxon clan living, father and uncles and aunts, hired men and hired girls, is already with the kings and queens of Shakespeare. And with them has gone an expansive and splendid American way of life that made each farm into a community, a small universe of justice and reward and retribution, that made poems of working men and rituals of common days. Marvellously complete and well-articulated farms, each a segment of civilization, with lifelong loyalties and loyalties and fealties beyond the grave, are lost now to the America they created. So much our progress by the machine has cost us. So much of our peace of mind and integrity and character has gone from us forever.

The empty barns, the few cathedrals that are left, are there on our horizons as savage warnings of what we are heading into, a world regimented and savorless, a world where farms decay, where men grow sterile and tired and rich, where men deteriorate and disintegrate.

Yet always, I believe—I *must* believe as a poet—some of

the older barns will last on the green carpet, in some green
corners of it, as on the hilly and rocky farms of Maine and
Vermont; there will be some, even if small, houses where
men and beasts and birds live together in partnership
through the years, face inertia and find themselves part of
a community of poems, keyed to the seasons, rooted in the
sun and the other stars, find a cousinship and wardenship
over creation; houses where men can find some affirmation
of a purpose, a plan, a goodness, finally, behind the farthest
fires of the final nebulae.

For no such beautiful buildings as these man has built to
take in the green year and keep it safe, in these our northern
places, can go entirely out of the world. And we shall still
have poems, probably, that come out of barns of our brotherhood with other creatures, out of barns of our cousinship
with the continuing creation of our universe. We shall probably have these houses for our salvation on this green carpet
of ours.

And in these barns we can still breed men of the breed of
Shakespeare, whose kings, when hard put to it, speak the
language of good shepherds and good husbandmen, whose
queens, in their extremity, think like housewives and house-
keepers and dairymaids and shepherdesses, and keepers of
flower-gardens. Sylvan men and women we shall rear, and
the goodly stock of the poets. For man exists not alone, but
only in the continuing economy of the grass and the seasons,
in the equity of green fields. Men like poems are metaphors.
They are metonymies, they are lively and lovely parts of a
great whole whose vastness we can see, in our wisdom, in our
poems, in common daisies in the grass, in the little frost-

[232]

flower on the edge of death and the snow. Barns are the breeding places of such metonymies.

Trust me, trust the poet: A man, like a poet, to be whole, must be a believer in the whole. A poem is a belief, if only for the golden length of its brief lines. It is belief in the act of life. And as such it can be the beginning of a religion, a religion better than theology can build, a religion of life. Barns, still, are full of the makings of such a religion. Even the brief, cold barns of today, empty of the sons who might have stayed on the green carpet but left it for the specious prosperity of the city. This late, a farmer, old and gray and tired, can stumble upon the cradle of Christianity and find the very marrow of our religion of good neighbors, of a loving father, of good will. On just another night of routine labor, in a cow-stall, he can come upon the recreating radiance where cattle stand mild in their straw.

Late Christmas

> He filled the lantern, lit the wick,
> It was so still he heard the tick
> Of the small death-watch in the wall.
> It didn't seem Christmas Eve at all,
> The house was empty as a shell,
> His grownup sons had turned out well
> And gone for good. Their mother lay
> Outdoors now by night and day.
> He took the lantern, got his pail,
> Took his coat down from its nail,
> And went out through the frosty shed.
> Christmas was gone clean out of his head,
> It was one milking time the more.
> The milking stool was by the door.

[233]

On the Green Carpet

He swung the door and raised his light,
And entered the midst of Christmas night.
Four damp legs and two big eyes
Tottered to meet him, friendly-wise,
Between the eyes as soft as silk
There was a star as white as milk
On the new young being there
Standing and staring its first stare.
A cow had been ahead of the mark,
Had come to her time there in the dark.
The man put down his light and knelt,
It might have been a child he felt,
The hair on the thin thing was so fine
To feel of in the lantern's shine.

VII

FOOTPRINTS ON THE GREEN

7. *Footprints on the Green*

And now, at the last, I should like to take time to explore a conviction that is never to be put adequately into words, since the words, it may be, do not exist, that can at best be hinted at, as the last and best virtue of the ancient and ever young carpet of the green countryside.

This exploration will involve a narrowing of my field still more, but I warned you that my circle was closing in and in as I went on. And if I narrow in, maybe I shall be able to go deeper. That possibility may prove a recompense to you.

I know you will excuse me if now, in this chapter, I become even more personal than I have been heretofore and have less to say about the great profession of poetry for the sake of the small profession of being and finding myself, finding myself as a poet, as a man. This effort will involve my going far back into my childhood and dealing with things that some adults might regard as the things that had best be put away with childhood as childish things. Yet any number of poets, Vaughan and Traherne, Blake and Wordsworth, to mention a few, and Scripture itself, are on my side in believing that retraversing the road of childhood is taking the highroad to the best understanding of the universe, with proper obeisance to the astro-physicists of today who declare we must unlearn most of our intellectual disciplines and language before we can conceive of the new discoveries on matter, that we have come upon so far. On this road the child, in a very substantial sense, is father to the man and also the best metaphor of all for the kingdom of heaven. For the child knows without knowing, believes without believing, and, without discipline of travel to a destination, is already there. The poet speaks very clearly about all this experience without experience he has had as a child:

The corn was orient and immortal wheat, which never should be reaped, nor was ever sown. I thought it had stood from everlasting to everlasting. The dust and stones of the street were as precious as gold; the gates were at first the end of the world. The green trees when I saw them first through one of the gates transported and ravished me, their sweetness and unusual beauty made my heart to leap, and almost mad with ecstasy, they were such strange and wonderful things. The men! Oh what venerable and reverend creatures did the aged seem! Immortal cherubims! And young men glittering and sparkling angels, and maids strange seraphic pieces of life and beauty! Boys and girls tumbling in the street and playing were moving jewels. I knew not they were born or should die; but all things abided eternally as they were in their proper places. Eternity was manifest in the light of the day, and something infinite behind everything appeared, which talked with my expectation and moved my desire. The city seemed to stand in Eden, or to be built in heaven. The streets were mine, the temple was mine, the people were mine, their clothes and gold and silver were mine, as much as their sparkling eyes, fair skins and ruddy faces. The skies were mine, and so were the sun and moon and stars, and all the world was mine; and I the only spectator and enjoyer of it. I knew no churlish proprieties, nor bounds, nor divisions; but all proprieties and divisions were mine; all treasures and the possessors of them. So that with much ado I was corrupted, and made to learn the dirty devices of this world. Which now I unlearn, and become, as it were, a little child again that I may enter into the Kingdom of God.

If you believe the poet here is talking poetry and not telling a history, if you doubt the *Bible,* make the acquaintance of any four-year-old child—you need not select a Traherne-to-be or a Pater-to-be—and he very likely will correct and convince you.

By the way, before I leave generals for particulars, I wonder if we realize that this elevation of the child to seerage is a very young thing in civilization. Its dewy dawn is in the Gospels; but its full dawn was delayed till the seventeenth century. I wonder, too, if we comprehend how revolutionary this doctrine of the potency and poetry of childhood is. It involves a sharp turn in a long road both in art and philosophy. It might well be that this is the most substantial advance since the *Republic* of Plato. It improves on Plato; it is an improvement on what mankind had come to believe were the unimprovable Greeks. The Greeks, in thought and art, ignored children as incomplete adults. There are few children in Greek sculpture or Greek poetry. The Greeks neglected their young. Now modern poets have corrected the Greeks.

If I had to put a name upon it, I should say this childhood experience without experience, this intuitive knowledge of childhood, is the experience of *oneness.* It postulates the overthrow of time and therefore the expulsion of death from the universe. It is a shrewd leap into the dark that turns out to be a leap into the loveliest of light, a light wider than space, undimmed by any night. I can believe in it thoroughly, not only because I am a poet but because I have also been a child. This right road I walked once, and this strange unmapped shining continent I visited once, long ago. I have been living, I think, as a poet in this place for many years. Suppose, now, I endeavor to draw up a map of its essential geography, as the essential preface to this chapter, before I go out to map later secret and holy places in this green carpet of our world.

It all began in childhood. Just how early I cannot say for sure. For the surer I grow of this continent that shines so clear in its features, the less sure I am of the matter of its years. That fact is an augury of vast import in itself. And with my growing conviction that the poet defeats time in his own lifetime and lives not only ahead into futures not his own but backwards also into pasts not actually or particularly his own, but maybe his father's, maybe his mother's, or maybe man's, I am all the more delighted at the prospect of having unheard of assistances in seeing this continent of mine clearer in poetry's memory than in my own mind's, of seeing it better now than ever I did then when I caught only glimpses of it, like a sudden high granite island seen through rifts of a Fundy fog off my Maine-world's coast. A poet deals in willful belief even with logic and science against him; this will to believe can work backwards as well as forwards, can recover lost truth, as well as that not yet conceived of. For it would be a deadly jurisprudence if man were not allowed to improve on his childhood as he is legally bound to do on his maturity, and on all mankind's!

It began, I say, long ago. I heard and saw things that have been like Autumn maples in sudden fire, burning without ever going out, as all trees in *fact* nature go out, without a falling of their leaves or splendor, on all my farthest horizons ever since. Believe me when I say these lights, in my dark seasons, are what have kept me going. Metaphor, as I keep insisting, is mightier than ordinary fact. This metaphor I use here is the physics of my being. Hence I am convinced that there is behind *fact* nature a deeper nature, a real. It shall be the business of this chapter indeed to establish this very poetic fact of a deeper and higher nature, superior to fact, a nature always creating or becoming, a nature of insistent good will, a nature of immortal will. For the proof of which I am going to take you now out on the particular corner I know best of the green carpet to show you certain deep footmarks which may point towards a meaning under and over this green carpet the world around, which is life itself to know.

As I say, I came on the first marks of this meaning, the prints of things like feet, in the brighter and brighter far reaches of my childhood. Here are some of them. I cannot hope I have recovered them all. More and more of them I hope to come on as I fare ahead being a poet into my future. To recover more of this splendid Lost Atlantis shall be the major principle of my being.

One of the first footprints—oh, one of the very first of all —is a sound. The sound of a bird. It was in the very middle of a dark night. I was sleeping beside my father, and that sound, going on over and over, woke me up. My tensing up to listen to it wakened my father. He knew my question before ever I asked it. My father was like that. He answered at once the question my tense small body by his was asking in the starry deep of the night:

The Rooster's Crowing

In the deep waters of childhood, in the deep
Waters of night, he came up wide awake.
A sound had come into him, not the sound
That made his father beside him throb and shake,
Not the sound in his father he loved so
To listen to and hear it come and go.

This sound was not like anything he knew,
It must be one of the things they called the birds.
It stayed a long time out there in the dark
And in him, too. It was much better than words.
His father woke up sudden and said, knowing
His small son's wonder, "It is a rooster crowing."

"What does the rooster crow for?" Father said,
"It is coming day. The rooster knows
The sun is on its way up through the dark,
The day is coming. So the rooster crows."
The man went back to sleep, but not the boy;
He lay there proud and taut with this new joy.

He had a father by him in his bed
Who even in the middle of the night
Knew where the day was, knew what the birds knew,
He had a father who was friends with light!
It would be good living with such a one
Who knew all the right answers to a son.

A cock crowing up the sunlight from under the earth . . .
Why should a rooster do that? Is the science of the thing,
the rooster's maleness, the whole science of the thing? Or is
there more? Is there some starry seed of light which starts

germinating and growing at midnight, and does the cock have sharp eyes to see that? Has the cockerel a golden right to sit on the top of our church spires and point out the unseen winds, and deeper facts than winds, facts like prosperity and trouble, coming life or death? Who put the bird there first, above the church, above theology? Is he holy?

Another very early sound I still hear just as it first grew slowly and gently on me. It was a wood-thrush singing across an evening. I was beside my father again. (So often the footfalls fell when I was with him!) The bird was deep in the woods, he echoed. Three separate songs, and each one went up a little higher than the other. So like clear crystal beads, so like liquid that tears welled in my eyes. It was my first thrush. Or was it one I had listened to for ages under that high forest there, my first woodland in this world?

A thrush singing in the woods. . . . It was the first bird I had ever really heard sing. It was a last marvel in a long chain of marvels. The first violets, like pieces of sky, the first anemones, like drops of snow left over into April. I had had my first trip out past all houses, out of sight of all windows and doors. I was too tired to take in anything more. Then, when the shadow of the earth was climbing up the eastern sky, the bird sang among the distant trees. Three broken little songs rising higher and higher until they faltered and failed. All at once I knew what it was to be alone and among things so lovely that they made your heart ache. For you could never tell how beautiful they were even though you were to live a thousand years and have all the best words on the end of your tongue. My father thought it was weariness that made me suddenly burst into tears. But it was the thrush.

And another time it was a rose, after all roses had gone and snows blew over the earth. I dressed early a Winter morning and went out and found it. I was not expecting flowers there, in December. But there the rose was, a vast white one made of driven, drifted snow. I stood in the center of it on frozen earth. A snowstorm during the night had heaped all of itself around the grindstone back of our woodshed. I marvelled then as a boy, and I marvel now, why dead snow had taken upon itself to spread itself in fluted lines in a circle around a common grindstone, a circle a small boy could stand in with the petals of the cold rose higher than his head. It must have been more than an eddying wind's and a grindstone's doing.

Still another flower of snow I came on and felt my heart come up against my ribs suddenly. It was in the upper pasture of Lost Paradise Farm, close to the old grass-grown cellar that always made my heart beat faster, it was so strange. It was Spring, yet here was a drop of snow hanging down from a stem among all the green April things there in a little glade. Fragile and white, it looked as if it would melt if you breathed on it. I did not touch it, I did not so much as breathe on it. I left it there, but it has not left me. It has been white in my mind ever since. It was not an anemone, it was too white and cold and heavy. It might have been a snowdrop. But snowdrops are cultivated flowers, and this was in the wild pasture. Who knows, though, but one tame flower might have survived from the house of long ago buried there under a green mound? Yet I wonder. It was not a bloodroot. I knew those blooms later on. It is too far north for them in Maine. So I still wonder.

Other childhood flowers burn and brighten in my mind. Not rare blossoms, roses of snow or a lost snowdrop, but common dandelions. But they were so thick together, they were so fiery that they sent up light high into the air, palpable, shimmering light. Like the gilt powder in my father's painting-box. You could see the light on the air. I was in my father's house, looking out from the dark into the day. That could account for some of the splendor. But not all. For that golden earth out there, for me, suddenly came alive, as though it were a tiger that had been sleeping and you thought he was dandelions on a blanket, and then all at once he stirred and was there. And that green field was alive for good.

Other tigerish flowers I recall seeing for the first time. Tall lilies hanging like bronze bells from rafters, dotted with rust, turned up at their golden rims. And they *did* ring. I heard their deep bronze sounds almost without hearing anything. And the carriage I was riding in went on past them, but I could still hear them making their bronze deep sounds for a long time, and it was not the sigh of the sand under our wheels. I have seen the tall wild turk's-turban lilies many times. Those flowers that rang may have been these lilies. But those first ones rang.

A carriage going fast . . . And I was in it with my father. All the pine trees each side were running backwards and out of sight. Yet suddenly I noticed that the tall pines away on the edge of the world were not running back. They were coming along with me and my father. They moved in company with us. They kept beside me. I knew—I was old enough to know—that trees did not move. But these tall ones did. And they are beside me still, moving out with me as we lift and rise on the carriage which is this world out among the tides of the stars. Anyone can see how distant trees do come along with one when he moves, while near trees rush back. And if those tall trees be high and beautiful enough, they will keep up with one just as surely as the stars in the sky.

Water high up through the trees . . . That was an early memory, too. I was riding with my father once more. It seems that those insistent sights and sounds crowded upon me always when I sat under the golden light in my father's sunlit moustache and under the twinkling light of his far-away blue eyes! It was through deep, dark spruces tall as the top of the sky. Yet through them, all their length from top boughs to lowest twigs, was light, sparkles of light, alive. Far lower down than even the road we were on, than my father and me. I asked my father what that light was. He said, the sea. I could not believe it. How could water be so far below the solid earth we were on, so high above? Suddenly we came out in the open, the trees fell away, and it *was* the sea—an entire mountain of running fire, like diamonds, far in under our horse's hooves, as we wheeled along the edge of a high shore, far, far above the white houses on a distant island. And white-sailed sloops were climbing up its steep side. That high blue of the sea could be higher than the world. It might be that even today we are moving by a wonder higher than the world, too, when we think we are going dry-shod on the small routines of day to day. We may be one with a vast whole we do not see because our eyes are too much on boughs near at hand. Those little white houses

on that island that day, those tall leaning sloops, did not
know what was over them, under them, always, like an
everlasting arm. There may be no up or down, no high, no
low, small or great, no parts really, but only one entire blue
peace and sureness, and we on it and in it and of it. We and
the graves of us on the headlands of the coast, we and all
sails and all coasts, safe like a bee in a blue morning-glory
too big for him to comprehend, looking for a little honey,
and not seeing how his blue flower is the universe wide and
entire.

It is haytime. The haystacks are there through the open
door. The sweet smell of them comes in. I am in the old
farmhouse. It is hot and yet growing dark under a most
brilliant sun. The haystacks are deepening in umber. All at
once I see why. High up a billow, worlds higher than the
world, is curling its white crest over the sun. It grows twilight time. The earth falls still. The sound of crickets comes
out loud as it does when the stars are coming out. The tall
popple tree by the door stops shivering in its silver leaves. I
know it is coming. And come it does. Or, better, it is there
as it has been forever. A tree purely of light, with rankling
twigs and tendrils by the thousands, terribly alive all over.
It comes and stands there, and it is gone at the same instant
for good. Our eighty-year-old popple against the tool-shed
there is gone. Only a silver stump of it shows on the deepening dark. It smokes, and sparks of light shed from it. It smells
like thick honey in the air. It smells like burning in the air.
The tree I had known all my life is nothing but a stump.
Over the house, shaking the house, the thunder instantly
rolls. I tremble, the timbers of the house tremble. And rain

as from a thousand split hogsheads falls and erases the farm.

I am still there. My tree is gone. Yet a handsomer, taller tree I had never dreamed of is there now, in me for good. My popple was only a slow dull guess at that tree. It is a part of that tree for good and all now. I am a part of it. I am not afraid. I had been afraid of thunder before, but never was I again after that. I have not been afraid of lightning since that long-ago moment on the edge of a July hay-day, on the edge of sudden bright death. The lightning I saw there was good. It was good the way the light was good in the eyes of my grandfather, dying on his bed, looking at me his namesake, his continuing self—I look very much like him, they say—for the last time. Who knows but that was the first time my grandfather knew who he was, and who can say but in recognizing himself so in that instant he escaped what seemed about to happen to him, about to put out forever the faded blue light of his eyes?

I have this journey back into childhood now to thank for two different experiences, which were once a part of my marrow and brain but which I had completely forgotten and might have lost forever, had I not gone on this journey just now. So I thank this journey for lighting up two scenes that had gone into darkness, and even more for joining the two experiences of light, which I had never connected before, into one lovely and continuing radiance that will be with me henceforth to the end and into whatever beginning there is beyond the end.

A night of vast storm there was also, shaking that same house of my childhood, and my father was standing by me, and, later on, holding me in his arms, by the light of a lamp or lantern or candle, and singing to me an old hymn, "I will stand by you until the morning." And I slept and listened to the song at the same time. And the morning came, and great pines and another of our old popples were down all around our farmhouse on every side, a felled forest around, roots and stumps tipped up like octopuses against the dawn. But our house was safe in the very middle of all the ruined trees, my father and I. And my father, or the hymn, or both, had kept a promise.

It was a dark November night, and I followed my father up a drear mountain of ebbed tide. We had no lantern, and needed none. For my father's feet made tracks of light on the rockweed there, and I could put my feet in their flame, and follow him home. I could not see my father, but I was sure he was there. And still is. For I swear there was more to that light then than phosphorescence. His footfalls were real fire to me that night, and they are so now. They are more of a real fire to me than the stars that circle over my house tonight; they will go out ahead of me into a wider dark. Though the house we were going to is dark now and my father gone, my father's feet of light go on still. They proved to me, for keeps, that there is a warden of small boys and small men warmer and older and younger than all the stars.

In my father's town house was a buck-deer's head with high antlers. I was immensely in terror of it. I never dared to enter that room by myself. For I was sure the wide-eyed thing would come crashing through the plaster from the room where his body was and trample me to death, if no one else was there. But that memory of fear has grown into a conviction that there was more than fear to that wild head. It

may be there could have been some haunting hunger for a
revelation of the secret of oneness behind all crazed and dying deer and all dying and sorrowing men. The deer might
have been trying to tell me that.

A Buck's Head on the Wall

Among my several memories of fear
The clearest is the farthest. From a wall
An antlered head stretched forth, and I was sure
An instant more the whole high wall would fall.

A great buck's body meant to move through trees
Would crash into the room and trample me
With hooves designed to cut the turf like knives
And eyes that stared and yet could never see.

I never went into that room alone,
And yet I found a way to hide the cause;
For I was early in perceiving how
People close their lips and fashion laws.

But now that I have played the game of law,
I like to think behind it to that head
Which towered from another universe
And filled my indoor's universe with dread.

And who knows but the great, mysterious shape
We feel has eyes on all the things we do,
Between the cradle and the grave, is such
Another sightless head, if we but knew?

Another such a head hung bodiless
Upon the walls we build to close us in,

While he who really is the one we seek
Goes far and lightly past the thought of sin.

Goes far and lightly, graceful as a buck
That dips his hooves in crystals of the dew
And never yet has bent his neck to come
Inside the walls his bright brain never knew.

And never yet has guessed his branching head,
As stately and as kindly as a tree,
Could come to be a symbol of a fear
To creatures who must bow to agony.

Death, we call it. But I have seen in the woods an intricately marked bird fallen deep in love with the more intricate markings on a snake swaying before his eyes, ready and eager to be slain, so rigid already with desired death that he let me hold him a moment in my hand after I had frightened the snake away. I am not so sure about death now. Maybe its music is a deeper thing than what we call life. Maybe it is like a hidden hand leading us in the gloom. I recall the blow my father gave me. The only one, ever. It stung me and numbed me. I was sure I would hate him always. I was sure he had died to me. Yet, though I can still feel that pain, I know now that the blow turned me for good from an act that was not good, that had death in it. My father may have died to me to make me more alive. A blow can be a death and a beginning.

Always, be it noted, it was on the green carpet, or towards the green carpet, that those fiery footprints in childhood ran. Where life had the color of green on it.

So let us turn now from the lost green continent of childhood towards the greener continent that childhood's may be the outpost, the metaphor for, the metonymy, towards footmarks that go on over the green world now, destined to a great destination, the footprints that may prove the timeless nearness and oneness of all things.

One poem I recall vividly is a poem made by footprints, three parallel sets of tracks going across a September morning, between the flowers of Queen Anne's lace, towards the sea and the sunrise. It was on my own meadow. The dew was so heavy the grass was entirely beads of light, and so the footmarks showed up as plain as three columns of darkness advancing through light to light. Who the people were who had gone that way, I never shall know. What they were after, I shall never find out. Why there were three people, and why the heaviest and tallest had gone in the center, as I could see he had, I cannot say. But I am just as certain there is a poem in those parallels drawn across the light. I am sure that some three men went out early one morning to the sea to meet the sun. And I know for sure that, whatever else they were doing, they knew they were taking part in a handsome poem that morning. Their tracks showed it. They had spoken to me in words printed in dew across the morning.

I have found other footprints towards the sun. And here are some of them.

Since I have spoken of an antlered deer in my childhood, massacred to become a metaphor for terror, it may be well for me to turn now first to my continuing experience with antlered deer, to my *Book of the Deer,* my book of the graceful children of the green carpet whose delicate flower-like feet leave many meanings on that green page, pointing to

[254]

some secret and deep good. My book has many chapters. Here are a few.

One chapter is a white doe so suddenly and arrestingly beautiful that she became almost a symbol of good luck or death. The people of the countryside longed, yet dreaded, to meet her; they did not know what the sight of her incredible slimness would bode them; yet they whispered the news when she had appeared. The hounds on the farms gave her a wide berth and left her unmolested. Even her own kind shunned her in the forest aisles and the frost-struck meadows. She went alone and lonely. Beauty, but it might be beauty like the end of earthly things. Maybe there is a footprint here.

Surely there are dark footmarks leading to light in a buck-deer that joined a herd of cows belonging to a man I know. Something must have happened to the wild thing; he turned tame. Maybe he was ailing. There were shameful and tabby days ahead of him. It was unholy for a thing that lives on air, free as the air, to come into slavery. The farmer did the only right thing there was to do.

Go Down Standing

Here in his pasture tamed two hundred Summers
An eight-pronged buck's high horns were on the sky,
The deer stood calm among the grazing heifers,
His only wildness was his rounded eye.
A forest thing wild as a hazel tree
Stood tame. It was a sorry thing to see.

Deer went this way, they said, when they were ailing,
Made up to men, went tame, came up to farms,

Forgot their old wild ways and trusted farmers
They hated once to keep them from old harms,
Grazed quiet with the cows at the woods' hem
And tried their best to be like one of them.

All day the man remembered and was bothered,
He hoped the antlered truant there would go
Back to his woods. But when the cows swayed homeward,
There were the high horns coming in the row,
Meek as the rest and with a slave's slow tread
Came one that wore the wildwood on his head.

The man remembered seeing a broken eagle
That needed the whole wide sky for his great wings
Eating the scraps that had been saved for chickens.
Fear and quick death were best for the wild things.
He should go down standing, this proud one.
The man went into the house and got the gun.

Certainly the footprints go towards light in another instance
I know, where a tall buck played the part an ancient cousin
of his once played in the tale of St. Hubert; he saved his
feathered kinsmen, the light woodcock. I know, I took part
in the poem in the role of Hubert:

> The hunter sensed his birds now in the briar;
> He raised his gun, his brain ran down to his sight,
> He drew his breath in deep. A sudden tree
> Towered above him, it put out his light.
>
> Half of his sky was gone, and he was small;
> The boughs of the tree above him were unleaved,
> Its branches leaned above him intricate,
> The tree was a high and warm one, the tree breathed.

[256]

Footprints on the Green

The man stood frozen, his fingers were brown ice
Under the branching gloom of the high deer;
Half a life away, on another world,
Three woodcock whirred to silence blue and sheer.

Such things must often happen in the deep pile of the green
carpet of the woods. A secret sympathy must league all wild
things into a burning brotherhood on the precipice of doom.
Wild blood is thicker than water. Brooks will tell tales, trees
will speak, birds will talk, wordless rabbits will cry out the
warning when the shadow lengthens towards mortality.
Sometimes the words come too late.

Too Late the Squirrel Laughs

Horror bristles the shivering pine,
The squirrel is frozen to brown ice,
Dark stillness has come over all
The snowy-bellied woodland mice.

Not a single crow to cry
The warning, but the cry is there
In the tense and terrible
Quiet on the frosty air.

Look up! look up!—The tree that moves!
Drink the wind with nostrils spread!
The hawk without the wings! The deer
That goes upright with hornless head!

Fear has cocked the delicate
Triggers in the rabbit's thighs,
The duck puts up her head, the fear
Rounds the ambers of her eyes.

[257]

Too late the duck runs up the air,
Her gold feet beating empty space,
Too late the squirrel laughs the laugh
On his taut unlaughing face.

The red bloom blossoms in the woods,
There is the high unliving sound,
It goes from tree to tree, it leaps
From hill to startled hill around.

Eyes going out as beautiful
As moonlight burning on hoarfrost,
And there are red drops on the leaves,
Wide antlers lying low and lost.

Creatures so graceful, so untamed, so shy yet gentle and
full of a natural good will, the slender deer, that grow handsome through hunger, whose life depends on their dream-
slim quicksilver feet, that live by the wisdom of a skin so
sensitive it thinks by itself, must hallow a tame place where
they pass and make memorable our common days by crossing through their sunlight. I know a common meadow on
our old farm, with tame golden pumpkins spilling from a
garden plot in it, that never was the same again after I had
seen how a mother deer and her young used that meadow
as their highway:

A doe would cross there slender and wide-eyed
With a song that was a slim fawn at each side,
Twelve feet without a sound, almost not there,
Three courtly cousins of the flowing air.

Footprints on the Green

Solemn as silence, the children of innocence
With heads high swam the light up to the fence,
Then at no sign they curved in effortless arc
Out of the light and into the forest's dark.

When such lightfooted ones are doomed to limp through the
short lean years of their life, surely then one can swear there
must be such a thing as unholiness in the world, evil as tangible as a bare bone. Ten thousand quiet brothers of the green
carpet must cry out in judgment on such a thing.

The Cripple

Cover your eyes with your hands. By the woodland pool
Is a sight too fearful for eyes to see.
A deep-eyed doe comes down the bank to drink,
Not on four lovely legs, but only three;
Her fawns come after her more timorous
Because such a cruel mockery can be.

Shaped on the airy anvil of the winds,
Edged to an innocent and flowing dagger,
This cousin to swallows and a running song
Must go on sorrow and a weary stagger;
Forever a dread will deepen her dark eyes,
The slowest hounds of fear forever tag her.

Wide aspen trees will clap green hands for wrath,
Slim balsams curse indifference of the skies,
Small finches beat the golden drums of their wings,
Tall herons stare with sadness for their eyes;
In every slim wild heart some spire of flame
Of ancient faith, each time she passes, dies.

On the Green Carpet

Pity the broken poem printed in turf
Under the halting hooves of this hurt doe,
Call for tears from the iron hearts of oaks,
So fleet a thing so slowly now should go!
Cry woe out to the thinnest edge of time,
And to the starry end of the world cry woe!

There are the *lachrymae rerum,* the tears of things, in such living dooms. There are such wounds even the healing, forgiving fellowship of the forest cannot heal.

Yet these second cousins to our cattle, these unregimented kine of the wild pastures have forgiven tame man's trespasses against them over and over, time out of mind. It is a poem men say they have seen happen in the woods. So gentle in wildness, these creatures must grieve at all cruelty of death even when it strikes down the tall two-footed creature they have learned so to fear. Clustered hoofmarks around an unhallowed spot write testaments of pity in the forests:

Forest Epitaph

They stand in terror round the thing. Their eyes
Are wide with golden fear at what is here;
Yet if eyes of the four-footed could,
These troubled wild eyes here would shed a tear.

Here lies the dreaded two-legged dangerous thing,
And there is nothing to it now to dread;
It lies quiet, it lies very low!
They sniff hair like their own upon its head.

They shake their thin high ears, they shake their horns,
They toss their heads and stamp their slender hooves;

Footprints on the Green

Its eyes are buried in the moss, the red
Stains are round it, and it never moves.

They wheel away, but turn again to it;
They know they ought to go and should be glad
A thing that brought such ruin to their kind
Lies so low. Yet somehow they are sad.

They grieve for it, it is so pitiful
An animal that once so fearfully stood
Lies cold as many of their kind have lain,
And in its ruin they feel brotherhood.

Strange and strong and evil as the ice,
Yet it is sorrowful such power dies.
They shake their heads, they cannot understand;
The deer stand round the thing with saddened eyes.

These marks slim feet have printed in this circle here are
surely words, fierce words if low, that tell insistently of an
eye that does not close behind the forest's glooms.

All wild things, so rightly sculptured by the wind and
want and fear, so exquisitely sensitive to life in their shaking
narrow hearts, know a language older and deeper than ours.
It may be that it is a tongue which was well known even to
men before the cities, the tall Babels of history, confused
tongues and shut men away from a language kin to the
soughing pines and chattering oaks, the thunder of steep
rivers, the thunders of waves on the seashore, close to the
universal language of dark and light, growth and decay. It
may be it is the tongue the stars and planets use for their
friendships out in the soundless abysses of space. Our birth-

right may have been sold for a worthless pottage when we
came out of the forests to live in the towns, when we quitted
fear and, in quitting fear, the beginning of wisdom, deserted
any number of bright-eyed deities. Our young children try
over and over to tell us so. Fear may be a food more suited to
the fellowship of divinity and mystery than our food.

Food of Fear

There is one beauty of the wild,
Another beauty of the tame;
A child, but never the young deer,
Can go beautifully, lame.

One of the beauties is as good
As the bloom on a girl's cheek,
The other shines on the spider's lines,
The hawk, the lightning's streak.

One is reiterate as rain,
The other single as last breath
And is its precious loveliest
A yard ahead of death.

The soft partridge leaps into it
When he leaps from the egg,
His life is the quickness of his eye,
The leanness of his leg.

A child has several ways to peace,
The fiery chipmunk but one,
He must go like quicksilver
To earth out of the sun.

Footprints on the Green

A man wooes over and over,
The horned buck but once
And is gone into untrembling trees
And the long silence.

Shyness is trivial on a boy,
It is the lifeblood of the deer
That feeds in all his slender days
On feverish food of fear.

I know I have seen a secret light that lingers on long after
the timid and kindly trusters in solitude and green loneliness
have arched their backs and sleek fur, or spread their rain-
bowed wings, and gone. I have seen the blue fire flash along
a heron's wings when he suddenly sensed dull human eyes
on him, pulled the triggers of his wings, and shot up to melt
into the blue sky. I had not moved a twig. I had stood still
as a tree drinking in the sharp unreal sculpture of necessity
and lightness. Yet wise and sympathetic videttes had been
there, and they had cried to the bird to be gone. I have seen
a flame not common this side of the sun on the brush of a
fox sailing across my road in my headlights at night. There
are such sudden fires.

I have seen shy infant partridges, huddled together with
their heads all out in the moonlight, know without sight or
sound the presence of me and death, and melt away into the
shadows they copied on their dappled backs. I have seen a
song-bird relax for one instant the bowstring of his being,
surprised by my gentle and kindly look upon him, gone in
an instant, bundled into a red ruin in the claws of a sparrow-

hawk, leaving only a feather floating in air. And I felt like Judas. I have, with my dull eyes, seen such slenderness and right patterns, learned from leaves, learned from the dappled sky, learned from the chevroned waves of the sea, on hawk and woodcock and whistler, that I felt guilty to be gazing at such providential beauty which was not made for any human eye to see, the casual and slow human eye. The myth of Actaeon is such a guilty conscience in man.

I know well there must be a supernal radiance behind these wise lights in little wild ones' eyes, on the great wild ones' velvet hide and horns. I have seen the right look at me from the scornful eyes of a moose, built by the same urgency as the gnarled spruce tree beside him, and there was no pity for so wrong a living thing as I was, so unlike any tree.

Such light of wild righteousness I have watched go out and leave a tameness only in eyes filled with the gentleness of death, watched fierceness and sufficiency and scorn fade pitifully:

The Pheasant

A pheasant cock sprang into view,
A living jewel, up he flew.

His wings laid hold on empty space,
Scorn bulged his eyeballs out with grace.

He was a hymn from tail to beak
With not a tender note or meek.

Then the gun let out its thunder,
The bird descended struck with wonder.

He ran a little, then, amazed,
Settled with his head upraised.

The fierceness flowed out of his eyes
And left them meek and large and wise.

Gentleness relaxed his head,
He lay in jewelled feathers, dead.

I do not think there is a more mysterious or more eloquent book than the vast and brilliant *Book of the Birds.* Some day, I hope I may write some chapters in it. I have been writing notes for them all my life. It is a book of such beauty that takes a man's breath. The colors are compacted of the rainbow and the flames of stars. In that book one can read the most amazing lessons. Lessons in cleanness and good will and courage, under soft feathers, that crumbles bronze. Birds are youth, it seems, and they never show old age or weariness. When weakness comes on them, they creep away to keep from making such shadows on the sunlit world. Birds are like a chemical reaction at sunrise; they turn from feathers and bones into a solar system of sounds. They have a will to live that is like arrows flying. The smallest birds assail the strongest hawks and drive them from their nests; the humming-bird turns a golden scimitar and swings a deadly arc over the hawk's cringing head. Young birds believe the world is the best world from the moment they open their eyes, and go on believing it in the beak of the hawk. Infant birds are decorous and patient in hunger. Robins have more sentiment than men; they mourn beside the ashes of the house where they nested and were born, refuse to mate, and

[265]

die of hunger beside the grave of their hopes. Justice is the mother and father swallows feeding their young in a sequence without a miss, without a hesitation. The *Psalms* and *Proverbs* of birds are without end. There is a *Bible* yet to be written, a Scripture all poets can feed on!

If to be slim and kin to the wind and sunlight is good; if to be quick and cousin to the thunder and go up in a thunder made by short wild wings is a virtue; if to be capable of quiet for hours and years is a wisdom; if to be aware to danger and a difference in the whisper of grass or the fracture of a twig; if to be able to be lonely and solitary and yet bubbling over with vitality is a goodness—then I have seen a thousand good footprints going on ahead of me on the green carpet, towards the sun itself, to a sun and sum of goodnesses behind the sun and the nebulae and all light. I have seen footmarks that must spell out an ultimate charity, a final unity, and an ardor to create through lovely designs the powers that can outwit death and undo all the consumptions of time.

Quiet and peace I know—all men know—are good. Being solitary is the beginning of strength, and a great good. And the forest and the meadow are the sole nations where peace and quiet and solitariness are the oldest laws of the land. These goods grow everywhere trees roof in a republic for foxes and thrushes and the deer. Study to be quiet, said old Izaak Walton, who lived aloof from the troubled years of bloodshed in his century in green pastures, beside still waters, angling.

Cruelty there is in the forest, along the green carpet; hawk headed home towards life with his victim's head hanging down in death, quicksilver weasels flowing along apple boughs towards innocent blind babyhood in down; yet this cruelty is one necessary to kind, a kindness that must include both the lion and the lamb. And behind the red death, no hate rankles; only innocence and a trust in a creator not always given the meek to know. Most birds must be devoured; yet they sing and flit debonair up to the deadly moment, and die in the midst of a song, forgiving life for being life. I have seen great innocence in the ambers of hawks' eyes as clear as in the eyes of young sand-pipers plunging into the endless ocean for the first silver fish caught by themselves. Perhaps the presence of innocence in both the fox and the crying hare is a footprint too bright with the dew of morning for our eyes to bear.

Mankind has always learned from the forest the laws of life, the laws of good shapes, the good shape, even, of God. In his childhood man identified himself with creatures, by totems of hawk-headed kings and bears, with beasts and birds. He has prayed to the bull to be virile; asked of the lion his tendons and strength; he has begged of the beaver his industry, of the eagle, his eyes. Today's young mankind, our children, still look worshipfully to the forest and the beasts, make friends with their swiftness and courage. I know a small boy who, for his best friend for five years, created a young wolf as his familiar, lived with him night and day, talked with him, went to school with him. His parents knew; his teacher well knew what a bright ally the boy had curled under his desk.

There is wisdom in the woods. We in our slow minds envy the quick-witted fox. We are sad for our loss of the ancient awareness to life still there in the creatures, the dexterity, the wild willfulness, the independence, the gaiety, the wholeness, their oneness with the place. All these were ours once, and we lost them. We also once were able to read the life-and-death language of the winds, to feel of the night, to know the straight right ways to love and food. We once thought in our bodies, in the muscles of our thighs and toes, before we shut up our mind in our brain. We once knew goodness was quickness; evil, being unaware. And these feathered and furred sons of freedom, we dimly guess now, are in close touch with poetry we have lost, with beneficences and benignities of the sun and the storm, presciences and salvations of the snow; the gnawing urgencies to love and live. Laws out of time, on no statute books save the rocks of the earth and the pressures of the tides and the silver knife-edge of the new moons. Loyalties out of space and hateful of death. Behind the deer and the song-bird, keeping them in song and gracefulness, there are magnificent materials for the making of scores on scores of great good gods.

Everywhere in the deeper greens of the green carpet there are these footprints that augur not only innocence and confidence in creation, but augur the existence of a oneness, behind both gentle and hard creatures, a togetherness forever untouched by change or time. And that is a clear slot that shouts how immortality has gone on ahead this way. We, the slow lovers and feeders on change that postulates decay, can have little conception of such great holiness as a life out of the reach of death. Yet there that life is, flying or running in fear from before us, in every green forest we enter.

O timeless innocence keeping a universe forever one brotherhood, a universe in which a mayfly's day is as good as the ten thousand of the turtle, forever young! Small wonder that children, sprung of such dewlit primal innocence, expect oneness of the world, expect their dogs to speak to them in a brother's tongue, make as much of a small dandelion in the grass as of the huge one in the sky, and guess at one untiring benevolence that knows where all things are, approves all things as good.

The very common sunflowers from their golden lips can cry out to us the truth, if we will not trust the mouths of babes and sucklings. The sunflowers know the kindliness and power of the good; they turn in their tough stalks to it, keep their heavy faces to the sun's face from dew-rise to dew-fall. The wild daisy knows how to keep its light in its eye by closing its eyelids tight in the dark. On the cool September slope of the year the blue frostflowers, like their white kin on the warm hill of June, make a shrewd guess at a god. They say he is in their gay image and cold to all life unless it be a burning eye like their own and his own. They make their guess, as we, ages ago as children of the race, as today's children guess, guessed at God's form as our own. And both the daisy and primitive man, and today's child, guessed right about the god. It *is* the sun, it *is* a man!—just as surely as it must run on the four slender and swift and sufficient legs of the deer, and plunge like the blade that is the taut hawk. For the One contains the All, and every metonymy and metaphor of fin or wing or feet or hands prove the presence and the shape that forms all forms, the shape beyond the change of shape, of a light beyond the death of light in all the suns and daisies that must burn out, quickly or slowly here, prove a light there, out of time, out of space, burning forevermore.

[269]

On the Green Carpet

One footprint more there is, deeper than all the rest, on the green carpet, pointing most fiercely towards the orient of all forms and shapes, dominions, powers, and principalities of existence. And the metaphor of the meaning of this deepest footprint is Will. It is not enough that there should be this secret federation, against time and change, of all created beings, that there should be a warm oneness that burns beyond the first and last stars. There must also be power that wills that this oneness be acknowledged by every living thing, even to the least, last sparrow; that this togetherness of all creatures, this secret metaphor of brotherhood shall always direct all creation to come, that the small circles forever be in the image of the great and return thanks for their wholeness to the eternal whole.

If any creature, if any man try to hide away from this insistence, and walk in the cool of his privacy, the hot archangel will seek him out and pronounce judgment on his sin of disobedience. No matter how tamely a man walk on the world, the wild insistence will come upon him from every creature, from every stone, from every side.

Strange Holiness

There is strange holiness around
Our common days on common ground.

I have heard it in the birds
Whose voices reach above all words,

Going upwards, bars on bars,
Until they sound as high as stars.

Footprints on the Green

I have seen it in the snake,
A flowing jewel in the brake.

It has sparkled in my eyes
In luminous breath of fireflies.

I have come upon its track
Where trilliums curled their petals back.

I have seen it flash in under
The towers of the midnight thunder.

Once, I met it face to face
In a fox pressed by the chase.

He came down the road on feet
Quiet and fragile, light as heat.

He had a fish still wet and bright
In his slender jaws held tight.

His ears were conscious, whetted darts,
His eyes had small flames in their hearts.

The preciousness of life and breath
Glowed through him as he outran death.

Strangeness and secrecy and pride
Ran rippling down his golden hide.

His beauty was not meant for me
With my dull eyes, so close to see.

Unconscious of me, rapt, alone,
He came, and then stopped still as stone.

His eyes went out as in a gust,
His beauty crumbled into dust.

There was but a ruin there,
A hunted creature, stripped and bare.

Then he faded at one stroke
Like a dingy, melting smoke.

But there his fish lay like a key
To the bright, lost mystery.

That this wild innocence is a holy thing, there are holy places by legions in the woods and fields to prove. All pagan races knew them. Christianity could but put saints' legends into these green and holy groves and wells of running water, to make them acceptable to theology. Many of them changed the theological hue back to their own good green color of perpetual youth, perpetual trust in innocence, eternal obedience to nature's will. Some innocent pagan tree of apples, a mysterious generosity from bare seeds which surround themselves with goodness to repay earth's creatures for sowing them in new fields—a mystery and generosity in the youngest apples still—one can be confident, is behind Milton's apples of disobedience. And the wild innocence has outlasted and obliterated the taste of the sin. The taste and fragrance of those ancient apples have made dust of Milton's theology and its narrowness. The apple of knowledge is not death, but life, as the fire Prometheus brought down from the gods of lightning, though it brought down on him the wrath and torture of a small, jealous, and all too human god, is eternally right and good. How else might it be, being of the same seed as the stars? The green carpet has triumphed. There can be no sin in apples, none in the wisdom of innocence. And the serpent, maligned and misrepresented by theology, winds innocently and eternally away in the righteousness of the shape that is he:

Whoever is responsible for this
Bitter law of hate come down so far
From dim ages better be ashamed
For my wanting to trample on a star.

Is it because a motion not his own,
But more like music, makes a man feel lame?
There was a time and place I went like this,
Like serpents, fish, and angels, without shame.

I myself came upon one such green-growing holy place as a boy on a Maine farm. It was in that green-grown cellar-place I spoke of at the beginning of this chapter, near where that white snow-flower mysteriously had sprung, and who can say there was no "understood" relation between flower and cellar? I knew the place for holy at once, and for good, without reason. There was no one to tell me, and I needed no one. One look told me. The spot was nest within nest of insistent metaphors, and though I did not know what metaphors were then, or what they were trying to tell me, I knew the place was a poem, and a poem about holiness.

Holy Well

One green spot in the pasture he knew well
Was holy. Something, any boy could tell,

On the Green Carpet

There was about this place. Here was a square
Wall of turf. A house had once stood there;
A hundred years of grass and the white clover
Had never been able to cover the cellar over.
It slanted down in one place steep and deep;
Never the merriest lambs among the sheep
Dared to venture into this breathless dell,
And what long years ago had been a well
Had gone back into wildness and a pool
With ferns curved over water, blue and cool
As the sky it came from, after the thunder.
But what was the node and heart of this deep wonder,
Was a briar-rose barbed fierce with thorns,
And it held up some long-dead deer's sharp horns.

Wild branches built by blood! And blood of the deer
Still ran in them among branches with clear
Rose-blood in them. Blossoms on this briar
Were pinker than the sky when set on fire
By Summer dawns. No other roses grew
So sweet or large as these. Yet the boy knew
He must never, never pick or touch them,
However much his fingers ached to clutch them,
Nor ever put his hot feet in that blue
Water there or brush those ferns that grew
Deeply over it. It was not right to do it;
He did not know the reason, yet he knew it.
Somewhere in old books he had read of a thing
That came over men at some pool like a wing
Of a great bird flying. By the water's side
They knelt bowed down in thirst until they died.

Those horns of rosewood, horns of deer-flesh, the water
from thunder on high, had all some secret understanding

[274]

together; they knew they were in a league of right loveliness. They all had run together into one flesh; that strange presence of the pool was as palpable as any angel ever was. And what was more, it insisted on making itself known. There was will behind its sincerity. And being still close to childhood, I had the power to know it without knowing, to see it without doubt.

Such fierce footprints as these point to the east, point to that fact that this green carpet I have been following leads up to the feet, the wings and the paws, the serpent and the rose-tree and apples, antlers of deer and thorns of roses, which are the One, the Good, the Eternal. Call him God, Jehovah, the Over-Deer, Overseer, Over-Serpent, Rose of Rose, Thorn of Thorns—call him a thousand good names; and he is all those good things behind those names, and he is lovelier and kinder than them all. For he is all kindness and tenderness, lord of the sparrow and the eagle. He is the creator of cruelty and tenderness, and the forgiver of them both. He sets the hounds free that follow the horned deer and hound him to sorrow; he stretches the tendons in the buck, lights the fire of terror in his eye; he bares the teeth of the hounds and knots their running thews; he runs on with deer and hounds to the bitter and beautiful end; to mortal pang and sharp edge of hunger, to life's swallowing up death, to the beautiful and bitter end. But that end is only the beginning of the circle that creates and loves and preserves all mortal deer and hounds, sparrows and men, sees the good in them all, and saves all the good of them always. Longer than light can reach, faster than light may travel, his creatures run on, always ahead of death, which is time, in the universe which is expanding circles of light. No sparrow falls but is safe; no deer dies but is recreated and remembered; no hound wearies but is renewed and made young. All together and all saved. *Togetherness.* The metaphor that mends and heals the world!

Crystal Moment

Once or twice this side of death
Things can make one hold his breath.

From my boyhood I remember
A crystal moment of September.

A wooded island rang with sounds
Of church bells in the throats of hounds.

A buck leaped out and took the tide
With jewels flowing past each side.

With his high head like a tree
He swam within a yard of me.

I saw the golden drop of light
In his eyes turned dark with fright.

I saw the forest's holiness
On him like a fierce caress.

Fear made him lovely past belief,
My heart was trembling like a leaf.

He leaned towards the land and life
With need upon him like a knife.

Footprints on the Green

In his wake the hot hounds churned,
They stretched their muzzles out and yearned.

They bayed no more, but swam and throbbed,
Hunger drove them till they sobbed.

Pursued, pursuers reached the shore
And vanished. I saw nothing more.

So they passed, a pageant such
As only gods could witness much.

Life and death upon one tether
And running beautiful together.

That will at the end, where the footprints end, as it is there
at their brave beginning, is the good father of all the brothers that fly, that creep, that run, that walk the green carpet.
Eternal sadness is his end, eternal joy. He saves all crystal
moments; he saves all trembling dying deer. The least daisy
is as dear to him as blazing Betelgeuse; he keeps both from
the dew-fall of death and tempest of time. All that moves on
the green carpet is his; the green carpet itself. He made it. It
is his living-room. It is the color of his mind. It is his promise
that there is a life which shall outlast the last stars, and
a community of brothers continuing in lovingkindness beyond the dark cankers of time. The footprints on the carpet
are his. His feet go on ahead to lead us home to his high love.

DATE